Thawing
Toxic Relationships

Don Carter, MSW, LCSW

DEDICATION

To my wife Angie, who has been my partner in so many ways
To the best children ever! Jennifer, Don III, and Brandon
And
To all those who desire to heal from the past and co-create healthy
relationships in the present

CONTENTS

Chapter 1

"What the hell is wrong with you?"

Comedian Bill Cosby has often observed that one of a child's most frequent answers to questions posed by their parents is "I don't know." He forgets to mention that one of a parent's most frequent questions to their children is some variation of *"What the hell is wrong with you?"* I always hated that question. How was I supposed to answer it? ... *"Well, Dad, I'm very happy you asked because I think we really need to talk about this. You see, my childhood dependency needs have not been getting met lately and, as a result, I am suffering from a pretty bad case of low self-esteem and some abandonment issues. If you could see your way clear to lighten up on me a bit I might have a chance to get back on track."* I doubt that would have gone over very well.

I am not sure that my alternative approach was much better for my own kids. I modified the question into a little game. When I found myself wanting to ask one of them, *"What the hell is wrong with you?"* I would stop, raise an eyebrow just a bit, look at them for a moment, and then curiously inquire, *"What grade are you in?"* They would give the answer to which I would smile and say, *"Oh ... that explains it! Maybe they don't teach you about this until next year."*

Motivation

Motivation has been defined as a drive, a need, a desire to do something. In human beings, motivation involves both conscious and unconscious drives. It is this writer's belief that people all have one *ultimate* motive in common. This motive drives everything we think, everything we feel, and everything we do from the time we wake in the morning until we go to sleep at night. I believe this motive is simply to be happy.

In this case, the term *happiness* does not necessarily refer to a feeling or emotion. Feelings come and go so it is not realistic (nor desirable) to hope to stay in one emotional state. Rather, used in this context, happiness is more like a universal *state of being* that describes and contains other states of being such as: contentment, satisfaction, fulfillment, completeness, and wholeness. Again, it is this *pursuit of happiness that is at the root of everything we think, everything we feel, and everything we do.* We all have this same ultimate goal in common, and we are all doing the best we can with what we have to get as close to that ideal as possible. If all of our efforts fail, and we move too far away from the ideal then things can go very wrong, as in the case of someone who can feel empty, unhappy, and unmotivated.

As our ultimate goal in life, the desire to be happy motivates us to make decisions based upon what will move us closer to the positive end of a continuum. On the negative end of this continuum is pain, something we try very hard to stay away from. Most of us do not like pain, but it does have a very important role in our lives. Pain is a warning system that tells us when we are moving in the wrong direction, taking us further away from our ultimate goal.

Granted, we sometimes purposefully make decisions that we know are going to hurt, in the short-term anyway. However, even these painful decisions are driven by the desire to be happy because we know that in the long run we will gain from the short-term pain. For example, deciding not to marry the person of our dreams until we finish college and get our finances in order may be painful in the short-term but very rewarding in the long run. It may even play a part in whether the marriage succeeds or fails. When we make decisions like this, we are said to be mature because we can delay gratification.

There are other times we make decisions that don't make us happy such as when we act without hesitating long enough to think it through. For example, impulsively taking out a new line of credit or buying a new car when we cannot afford it may provide some instant gratification but soon leads to buyer's remorse and other negative long-term consequences when the bills start coming in. Buyer's remorse is an example of an emotional consequence we suffer when we realize what we have done and how it is going to lead to our future unhappiness. When we don't stop and think it through before we act, we are said to have impulse control problems, a sign of immaturity.

When immaturity persists into adulthood it suggests that some sort of developmental delay has taken place such as emotional arrest. Developmental delays are usually the consequence of unmet childhood needs. Frozen feeling-states are another way of describing these developmental issues. We will explore these concepts in great detail throughout this book. We will also explore a very simple, yet incredibly powerful formula, A $\rightarrow$ B ($\rightarrow$ = leads to). This formula is where A is a choice we make and B is the outcome. The outcome is where we find ourselves on the pleasure and pain continuum as a consequence of our choice.

Maslow's Hierarchy

The American psychologist Abraham Maslow (1968) devised a six-level hierarchy of needs that, according to his theory, drive human behavior. I believe that each of these needs must be met in order for one to truly be happy. Maslow progressively ranks human needs as follows:

1. Physiological - food, shelter, clothing;
2. Security and safety;
3. Love and feelings of belonging;
4. Competence, prestige, and esteem;
5. Curiosity and the need to know; and
6. Self-Actualization

Maslow suggests that each preceding need must be met, at least to some degree, before one can go on to the next level. For instance, a child may not be able to pay attention in class if she is preoccupied with hunger. Maslow refers to the first four levels as deficiency needs and the last two growth needs.

While these needs are important for all human beings, special attention must be given to how we meet these needs in children because, as we shall see, it is the meeting of these needs, or not meeting them, that sets in motion a whole series of events that have an impact on the adjustment of that child. In children, deficiency needs are also referred to as dependency needs because children cannot meet these needs themselves; they *depend* upon their caretakers to meet these needs for them.

Childhood Dependency Needs

Small children cannot meet their own needs, much like a plant cannot water itself. As we grow, we become more *independent* and able to meet more and more of our needs on our own. There are two groups of dependency needs. The first group is the survival needs. These are what Maslow calls the basic needs for food, shelter, clothing, medical attention, safety and protection. If these needs are not met, at least to a minimal degree, the child is likely to die. Notice that the survival needs include the child's need to feel safe and protected. If a child does not feel safe she cannot relax. She is always on guard, scanning her environment for danger. Her anxiety level is very high, and she has to stay alert and "tuned in" to everything going on around her causing her to become hyper-vigilant, hyper-alert, and/or hyper-sensitive. Feeling safe helps children relax; if they can't relax they can't play. If they can't play it interferes with their growth. Play is how children learn and grow along normal developmental lines.

Because feeling safe is so important, children have a built-in psychological defense mechanism called idealization which functions to help them feel safe. This is necessary for them to be able to relax enough to play which, again, is the business of being a child. Through idealization, children (not referring to teenagers here) set their parents up on a pedestal, seeing them as godlike creatures. This makes them feel safe because "if I am protected by a godlike creature and then nothing can get to me" (Bradshaw). Of course children cannot yet think that way, but they "get it" that way in an emotional sense. We will come back to idealization later.

The emotional dependency needs are what Maslow refers to as the basic needs for love and esteem. These are the needs that nourish a child emotionally. If they get these needs met fully on a consistent basis, children thrive and flourish. If they don't get these needs met, they suffer to an extent proportional to their lack of need fulfillment. John Bradshaw (1992, 2005) refers to the following as primary emotional dependency needs: *Time*, *Attention*, *Affection*, and *Direction*.

Time = Love

Bradshaw and others point out that a small child equates time with love. In his video *Shame and Addiction*, Bradshaw states, "Little kids get it that whatever their parents give their time to is what they love." So if dad is gone working ten to twelve hours a day, which may be his way of showing love, the kids feel that dad loves what he is doing more than he loves them. They don't understand about budgets and bills. They don't understand that this may be dad's way of demonstrating his love for the family. All they know is he is usually gone and when he comes home, he is too tired to spend time with them. All he wants to do is rest, read the paper, and watch some TV. The main point here is that the children need time from *both* parents, not just one. They need enough time from each parent to get the message that they are loved as much as anyone else in the family. It is not as much of a question of quantity as it is of consistency and quality. "Quality time" is when the child's other three emotional needs are also being met.

Attention = Worth

Just as children equate time with love, they get it that attention equals worth or value. Attention is more than just listening to the children; it is *attending* to them. Parents attend to children when they take them seriously, show genuine concern and curiosity about who they are, what they think, how they feel. Attentive parents notice when the child is struggling with a feeling and help figure out what it is and what to do about it. They are engaged in their child's life, to the extent that they know how their child's day went, who the child is hanging out with, what the highlight of the week was, etc.

Children need lots of attention, and if they don't get it their behavior becomes attention-seeking. This is not deliberate on their part. Most of the time, children really don't know why they act-out in ways that are obviously designed to get attention. They are compelled to do it because they *need* attention, not because they *want* attention. When was the last time you heard this statement, "Oh, he's trying to get attention, just ignore him." Sometimes this is bad advice, other times it is not. There are two reasons kids show attention-seeking behavior: when they are not getting enough attention, and when they have been used to getting too much attention. The latter will be discussed when we look at the need for direction.

Affection = Approval

As a therapist, it has been my experience that affection is the area where many families seem to fall short. Many of my clients have told me, "Well, mine were not the most affectionate parents in the world, but I always knew they loved me." I am sure it is true that they were loved. However, I am also aware that kids need hugs, kisses, pats on the back, and words of encouragement on a regular basis. Displays of affection are how approval messages are sent from the parent to the child. Affection says "I like you," "I like who you are and who you are becoming," "I am glad you are my child," I am happy I get to be your parent," "I am grateful we have been blessed with you." In other words, affection is how children get the message that they are approved of by the parent. How many of us know a child who is not sure what his father thinks of him? Or one who is uncertain whether she measures up to her mother's expectations? How many are sure that we *don't* measure up?

Kids who don't get enough affection display approval-seeking behaviors such as people-pleasing. They act-out their need for approval by trying to please mom or dad. When their attempts go un-noticed they try harder and harder to please them, setting in motion the development of an ingrained pattern of people-pleasing behavior. We will look more at these types of behavioral patterns later.

Direction:

Guidance = Competence

Children are born not knowing how to do things. They are biologically programmed to survive in the wild, but everything about how to live in our culture must be learned, including relationships. Our caretakers are our teachers. Dad shows us how to be a man in the world; Mom shows us how to be a woman in the world; and they both show us how men and women get along with each other. In other words, our cultural and interpersonal programming is not biologically endowed but comes through the modeling of our parents, whether they realize it or not.

In the ideal situation, parents do realize the powerful influence their behavior has on the development of their children. They also know that to be good teachers they have to be available and approachable: i.e., the children know when and where to find dad or mom, and they know that it is okay to go to them for advice and assistance. To be available goes back to the issues of time and attention, parents must make the time to attend to the questions of their kids. To be approachable they must also be patient, tolerant, and affectionate. Good teachers understand that kids need repetition to learn. They may have to ask and be shown more than once in order to develop competence at a certain task.

A sense of competence and mastery are critical to the development of a child's sense of self. For instance, when parents teach a child to ride a bike, they hold on and hold on until the child gets her balance, and then they let go. Usually, the child will crash a time or two, but soon she takes off and rides. Did you ever see children who take off on a bike for the first time? They light up like a Christmas tree and almost universally shout the same thing: *"Look at me! I'm doing it!"* This is a statement of competence and provides a huge boost to their ego. After a while, you might hear the same child shout, *"Look at me! I'm doing it with no hands!"* This shows that the child now has a sense of mastery. Do you ever wonder why kids do the same thing repeatedly once they become proficient at it and avoid things they might not do well? Satisfying the need for a sense of competence and mastery is the reason. Children need as many I-can-do-it experiences as we can give them. Things like tying their shoe for the first time, driving a car, going on a date, learning to dance, getting good grades, learning to cook, hitting a baseball, etc.

Parents help their kids get the I-can-do-it experience by helping them develop the skill sets necessary to perform a given task. This again requires time, attention, and affection. If children learn the fundamentals of something, they are much more likely to succeed. If they try to learn on their own, without any ideas of the fundamentals, they are likely to fail more times than they need to. Kids who fail too much eventually give up trying. They need available and approachable teachers to help them learn.

Approachable teachers help without resorting to criticism when working with a child. It is truly an art, and most of us were raised on criticism so it is difficult to learn. Healthy critical feedback comes with love, tolerance, and without shame. For example, helpful criticism might sound like this: "I know it's difficult." "You are doing very well …I fell off more than this when I was your age." "I know you can do it, let's try one more time for today." Shameful criticism sounds like this: "Oh come on, don't be a big baby!" "You always make things harder than they should be." "Your brother took off on his first try … are you going let him make you look bad?"

One other issue regarding guidance is *over-protection,* which must also be explored here. There are some families that have rigid, sometimes extremely over-controlling rules designed to "protect" the child. For example, "The training wheels don't come off until you are twelve years old," "You cannot climb trees," "You can go outside but don't do anything," and "You must wear a football helmet if you are going to get on the swing set." They also do everything for the child, even that which children should be able to do themselves. Over-protection and over-involvement is a result of a parent's inability to tolerate any chance that their child might get hurt, physically or emotionally (failure). This can easily be mistaken for love, when, in fact, it is not. This is more about the parent's need to feel safer than it is about the child's need for protection. The child not only misses out on the I-can-do-it experiences but also gets a message from the god-like creatures in his life that *he can't do it*–a feeling of incompetence is the result. The child feels *"If Mom and Dad don't think I can do it, then I must not be able to do it."* These kids usually end up with all kinds of problems with indecision, shame, fear, and anxiety.

Discipline = Character

Discipline is the second form of direction kids need. Children are born without the internal structures to control their own impulses. Therefore, they were given external structures, called parents, to help them. When parents set limits for their children they are telling them "Here's the line, if you step over it this is what happens" (A → B). Setting and enforcing good limits helps develop the internal structures necessary for children to control their own impulses. These structures build character. Character consists of two primary internal structures: *values*–the knowledge of right and wrong, and *self-discipline*–the ability to delay or deny the gratification of impulses based upon that knowledge.

If we remember a simple formula, A → B, then we will have quite a bit of knowledge about setting good limits. Cause-and-effect seems to be a law of the universe. Simply put, when our *behavior* (A) is a good thing, then the *outcome* (B) should also a good thing; when A is a bad thing, then B should also a bad thing. The consequences we receive (positive or negative) shape our behaviors by reinforcing the good and dissuading the bad. While this formula is simple in theory, it is difficult in practice because this life does not always go as it "should," as we shall see in the next chapter.

Healthy limits are firm, effective, and consistent. The limits (B) are also connected and proportionate to the behavior (A); i.e., let the punishment fit the crime. When parents set and consistently enforce good limits for their children, they are teaching an important law of the universe. This will be extremely significant to children later in their adulthood when life becomes their teacher. Conversely, when we are inconsistent with the limits, or they are inappropriate for the behavior, then we are doing our children a huge disservice. For instance, when a teenager does "A" (e.g., comes home smelling of alcohol), and they should receive "B" (e.g., grounded for a certain period of time) but the parent feels sorry for them because the prom is this weekend, so they provide "C" (Letting them off the hook and giving them $50 to have a good time) then the message sent and received is A → C, In other words, "If I screw up when it really counts, Mom and Dad will bail me out." Providing "C" when "B" should follow interferes with the grand design, *enabling* problem behaviors to persist.

Decisions about good limits are not always easy. Some limits must be nonnegotiable, e.g. those related to the safety of the child and those connected with strongly held family values, while others can be structured to teach the child flexibility and how to compromise. For example, when the child does "A" (breaks curfew by thirty minutes *for the first time ever*), and the agreed upon consequence is "B" (grounded for the next two weekends) the negotiated agreement might be that the child can choose which two weekends of the next month to be grounded.

Another word for limits is boundaries. When parents set and consistently enforce healthy limits, they are helping their child learn healthy boundaries. Children who don't know where the boundaries are tend to feel unsafe. Spoiled-child syndrome is what results when a child is given blanket approval for everything he or she does. When there are little or no consequences provided for these children, they push the limits and push the limits until someone steps in to say "no!" Misbehavior in this case is *discipline-seeking* behavior. The child is unconsciously acting-out his *need* for help with controlling his impulses, and they are compelled to get it. Just as in over-protection, the well-meaning intentions of the over-indulgent parent backfire. Usually, the parents are trying very hard not to hurt the child's self-esteem with criticism, so they rarely provide this form of protection. The child gets the message that the god-like creatures in his life have no expectations of him because they are not capable of living up to any expectations due to incompetence.

Other forms of discipline include the ones that moms and dads model for us in their own daily behavior, including good manners, hygiene, work ethics, etc. We watch and learn from them. The old adage *"Do as I say, not as I do"* is not very effective in helping our kids develop and internalize these daily disciplines. The most effective tool in teaching kids is good role-modeling. Limits and consequences simply reinforce what we demonstrate.

The Iceberg Model

Throughout the book, I will refer to *the Iceberg Model* [Fig.1] to develop a picture or roadmap of what happens when childhood dependency needs go unmet. The Iceberg Model has been used as a visual tool to simplify very abstract concepts of being human by many people, including Sigmund Freud, Friel and Friel, and Dr. Larry Crabb, to name a few. You will hear many of the ideas and principles of the pioneers in the field of addiction theory such as Charles Whitfield MD, John Bradshaw, Pia Mellody, Vernon Johnson, Claudia Black, Terrence Gorski, and many others. They have been my teachers on such topics as addiction, codependency, Adult/Child Syndrome, abandonment, shame, and childhood dependency needs. I have used the Iceberg to integrate some of their ideas, along with many of my own, into this unified model of the issues underlying most addictive, mental, emotional, interpersonal, and even spiritual problems. To delve deeper into many of the concepts presented here see Appendix A for a list of suggested readings.

It has been my experience that most people have a profound revelation about who they are, where they came from, and where they can go from here after hearing the Iceberg lecture. It is my hope that this book will produce the same results for you, the reader. Again, the best thing about this model is that it keeps some very abstract ideas relatively simple and provides a concrete roadmap for understanding and preparing for change. So let's get started …

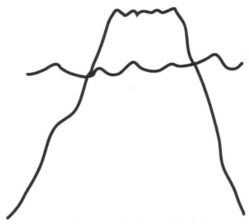

Figure 1: Iceberg Model

The Iceberg represents a human being. The waterline represents the dividing line between what is in our consciousness or awareness (above) and what is in our unconsciousness or our unawareness (below). The deeper one looks beneath the surface symbolizes the deeper we are into our unawareness or our unconscious. It is my hope readers will have a better idea of how to achieve that one "ultimate motive," which we all have in common by the time they have finished reading.

Please, if you are a parent, as you read, try to focus on at least as much of your own childhood experience as you do on the experience of your children. This book is not about blaming parents because, as we shall discuss later, the vast majority of parents do the best they can with what they are given. If you are reading this book, chances are that sometime in the past you have said something like, *"My kids are going to have it better than I did!"* This statement is an affirmation that you understand what it is like not to get your dependency needs met, at least to some degree.

Chapter 2

Anatomy of an Emotional Wound

According to Linn, Fabricant, and Linn (1988), in the early 1900s if you were born into an orphanage in the United States you were likely to be dead by the time you were two years old. This was according to a study done by Dr. Henry Chapin, a pediatrician in New York City. There was another pediatrician, Dr. Fritz Talbot, who found those statistics unacceptable. He discovered an orphanage in Dusseldorf, Germany where the mortality rate was the same as the general population, so he went to investigate. The doctor found that the orphanage followed very similar policies and procedures as those here in America with one small difference. There was an older woman named Anna, who carried a child on each hip. The director of the orphanage told Dr. Talbot, "When we have done everything medically possible for a baby, and it is still not doing well, we turn the child over to old Anna. Whenever a child cried the woman would pick the child up, hold him or her, and give motherly love. A few minutes with old Anna literally meant the difference between life and death for some kids."

When this doctor came back to the United States, he shared his findings and several institutions recruited volunteers to do the same things Anna did. Not surprisingly in a very short time the mortality rate quickly became consistent with the general population.

Abandonment

Children who get their dependency needs met fully on a regular basis will thrive, flourish, and grow at a healthy pace. Life will be good for these kids. In the worst-case scenario, kids who do not get their needs met at all will experience a failure to thrive, and many will die. Let us use the analogy of an emotional gas tank; if our needs are met fully we feel full, complete, satisfied, content, and happy. If we don't get our needs met at all we feel a great emptiness inside. I have heard this emptiness described in many ways: a black hole, a void, a vacuum, an ache, or a longing. Perhaps we get our needs met half-way; we feel half-full but something is missing, and we still feel an ache. These are emotional wounds, also known as *original pain*, and they result from an *abandonment* of our childhood dependency needs.

A Word about Blame

When parents do not meet the needs of their children, it is not usually because the parents don't love them. I say "usually" because there are those cases that one cannot understand, accept, explain, or excuse for any reason. However, most parents do the best they can, given the internal and external resources they possess, to take care of their children. In fact, I cannot count the times I have heard parents say, "I try hard to make sure my kids have it better than I did." This speaks very loudly to me. It says that these parents are familiar with unmet dependency needs. So, most often, it is not the parent's lack of love or effort that is to blame. It is usually because of one of the following reasons that abandonment occurs:

1. Circumstances: For example, if one parent dies and the other must take two jobs to care for ten children, circumstances are to blame for this, not the parents. None-the-less the children get hurt in the process.

2. Wounded people wound people: Parents cannot demonstrate much more than they have been given. Our parents were raised by their parents who likely were also wounded, and

they were raised by their parents, etc. Maybe dad is an alcoholic; he has a disease that impaired his ability function in his major life roles, including his ability to be the kind of father his kids need him to be. He did not aspire to become alcoholic. Alcoholism chooses you, you don't choose it. Perhaps mom is so chronically depressed she can't leave a dark room much less take care of anyone else; she didn't choose that. However, the primary issue for parents is that they are wounded themselves, sometimes moderately, other times severely because their parents were also wounded, and their parents were wounded, etc. Whatever the issue, the result is wounded children.

Again, it is not usually a question of whether our parents loved us, or even if they did the best they could for us. Many people get stuck on this truth and end up saying, "So why go back and dig all that up? They did the best they could and that is that. You can't change the past." To those people, I say keep reading, this book will show you why it is important to "dig all that up." Suffice it to say here that assigning blame is *not* the reason.

Children have not yet developed the skills to cope effectively with emotional pain. It seems they can handle a broken arm better than a broken heart. They rely heavily on a defense mechanism called repression to push the emotional wound deep into their unawareness [Fig. 2]. They also act-out their pain in various ways as a survival instinct which calls attention to it so the adults in their life can assess, diagnose, and respond to them. If the adults are unresponsive, and the child continues to experience abandonment the wounds accumulate.

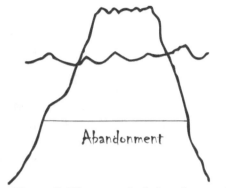

Figure 2: The wound of abandonment

The extent of the wounds may be mild, moderate, or severe depending upon the extent of the abandonment. Mild to moderate cases of wounding comes from situations in which the child does not fully or consistently get their emotional dependency needs met. There may be few overt signs of family dysfunction or abuse. For instance, it may be that one or both parents are able to give reasonable amounts time, attention and direction but are unable to express affection. The words *"I love you"* may rarely be heard, if at all, in this family. A lack of hugs, kisses, and other forms of emotional warmth leave a child to wonder how they measure up in the eyes of their parents. It makes matters even worse when the child lives in a shame-based family system. In such families the children get messages of disapproval through constant criticism rather than messages of approval and warmth.

A shame-based family system is characterized by the parent's use of shame to provide direction to the child. For instance, when a five-year-old child scrapes his knee the parent, or parents, might tell the child to stop crying because *"Big boys don't cry."* They may also simply ignore the child until he or she stops crying. Similarly, when the child makes a mistake the parent might say, *"What's wrong with you?"* or *"Why can't you be more like your sister?"*

Sometimes the shaming goes to extremes, especially when a wounded, shame-based parent is angry: *"You are going to end up in prison!" "You'll never amount to anything!" "You never were any good; why do you do this to me?"* These comments are often accompanied by slaps or even punches from the parent. In shame-based families these types of comments and behaviors are often intended to "help" the child learn right from wrong. However, while the intended "help" may actually produce the intended result the next time, another result is emotional wounds for the child. Shame is discussed in more detail in the next section of this chapter.

Another common abandonment scenario occurs when one of the parents is physically absent much of the time. The parent may be a "workaholic" who cannot seem to stop working long enough to find time for his family. The workaholic rationalizes his absence and breaks promises to be there for the child in the same way an alcoholic rationalizes her drinking and breaks promises to stop or control it better.

By now, the reader may begin to suspect that abandonment and wounding must happen on some level to most, if not all, of us. I believe it is true that all of us experience emotional wounds in life, but *not all of us* experience abandonment. The best example is when we lose someone or something important to us. Grief is a natural part of living, and one cannot escape an encounter with it for long in this world. When someone or something becomes important to us, we bond with it on an emotional level. Emotional wounds result when this bond is breaking or broken. Grief is the process we must go through to let go of the attachment and heal from the resulting loss-related emotional wound.

The absence of a parent may be perfectly justifiable as when a military parent is abruptly deployed overseas for a year or longer. As already mentioned, little kids get it that parents love what they give their time to. So if the child gets little or no time from a parent, the child tends to *experience it* as little or no love, regardless of the reason for the absence. Whether or not it results in abandonment in the case of circumstantial, unavoidable, or justifiable absences, such as the above example of deployment, is determined by what happens before, during, and after the absence of the parent.

There has been much written that suggests the terms "abandonment" and "loss" are interchangeable. While both result in emotional wounds, the author believes they are not interchangeable terms and that an important distinction must be made. *Abandonment always involves loss for the child, but loss does not always involve abandonment.* Loss-related wounds can heal if the person possesses the psychological support and emotional coping skills necessary to aid in the grieving process. Children who have emotionally healthy, responsive parents tend to get their needs met consistently. Because of that, they are equipped either internally with their own coping skills (depending on their age) and/or externally with parents who are able to provide the necessary support through the grief process.

When children cannot put into words what they are experiencing, whether it be from abandonment or other significant losses, their pain must find expression somehow and does so through *compulsive* patterns of behavior commonly referred to as "acting-out." When their needs are going unmet, children are *compelled by instinct* to act-out their needs through behaviors designed to elicit an appropriate response from caregivers, provided the caregivers are able to respond appropriately. If it is attention he need, the child's behavior will be attention-seeking. If they need approval, the behavior will be approval-seeking. And if the child needs discipline his behavior will likely be discipline-seeking. It is as if the child is an actor in a play, hence the term "acting-out." There are some clearly defined patterns of acting-out that not only help children find expressions for their pain but also actually help them to survive. We will discuss these patterns of behavior, better known as survival roles, in greater detail in the next chapter.

As already mentioned, young children do not possess the necessary skills to cope with emotional pain on their own. As with everything else they are dependent on their caretakers for help in grieving. The best children can do is to act-out their pain and hope their parents and other caretakers in their lives are healthy enough to notice the behavior, accurately assess the need, and respond accordingly. When parents possess the skills to respond consistently to their children's needs for time, attention, affection, and direction, they are helping their children resolve the current episode of grief to some extent, as well as to build the internal structures necessary to cope effectively with grief and loss on their own later in life. When parents are not able to respond appropriately to the child's need for help, loss-related wounds tend to accumulate right along with the wounds of abandonment, further complicating the child's pain.

Severe cases of emotional wounding, also known as trauma, results in situations where children have experienced overt abuse or other major losses coupled with inadequate support to aid in their grief. The emotional trauma that comes from abuse violates not only the child's emotional dependency needs but also his most basic needs, the survival dependency needs. This is especially true for their need to feel safe and protected. Imagine a child's dilemma when he needs protection from the very people who are supposed to provide it. The following are some forms of abuse and/or major losses that produce moderate to severe emotional trauma in children:

Sexual and Physical Abuse

Emotional abuse or neglect: Emotionally unavailable parent(s) or parents who give their child the opposite of what they need such as name-calling, belittling, threats of abandonment, shaming, etc.

Psychological abuse: Ignoring the child as if she does not exist or denial of a child's reality such as telling her they didn't see what she saw (e.g., "Daddy wasn't drunk, don't you ever say that again!")

- Frequent Moves
- Adoption Issues
- Prolonged separation from a parent
- Reversal of parent/child roles
- Rigid family rules
- Divorce
- Death of a parent or other family member
- Mentally Ill parent or family member
- Cruel and Unusual punishment: such as locking a child in the closet.

Shame

As discussed in Chapter 1, it is imperative that children feel safe and protected as part of getting their survival needs met. In order to feel safe, even in an unsafe environment, children idealize their caretakers. In other words, little kids put their parents up on a pedestal and see them as perfect, all-knowing and all-powerful god-like creatures. Idealization is a defense mechanism that helps children feel safe because they get the feeling that nothing can get to them, since they are protected by a god.

Since god-like creatures are perfect, they are beyond reproach in the innocent mind of a child. Children cannot say to themselves, *"Well, Dad has a drinking problem. That's about him not me; I don't have to take it personally when he breaks his promises and yells at me all the time."* No, in the mind of a child it goes more like this: *"If I were a better kid Daddy wouldn't drink."* or *"If I was a better kid Mommy wouldn't yell at me so much."* or the classic, *"Daddy, please don't leave, I'll be good!"*

Because of idealization, young children can make sense of it no other way; it has to be about them. Parents have all the power, and the child has none. They are totally submitted and committed to the parent. Thus, they develop a sense of defectiveness, and it begins to grow along with the wounds. So, if abandonment is an emotional wound, then *shame is an emotional infection* that sets in as the wound goes unattended [see Fig. 3]. This infection has a voice, and it grows stronger as the wounds accumulate. The child's self-talk begins to sound like this, *"No one could ever love me." "I don't count." "What's wrong with me?" "I'm stupid, lazy, unworthy of anyone's attention."*

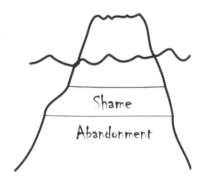

Figure 3: The infection of shame

In a shame-based family system, these internal messages of shame are actually confirmed by the parents. Sometimes the confirmations are more subtle and come in veiled threats of abandonment, double-bind messages, gestures that convey contempt for the child and other nonverbal expressions of disdain. Other times the confirmations are directly stated through name-calling, belittling, and emotional battering such as *"You're stupid, ugly, lazy, fat,"* etc. *"No one could love you." "You can't do anything right."* These messages result in what John Bradshaw (2005) has termed "toxic shame" in his book *Healing the Shame that Binds You.* Of course, these messages frequently come with a misguided positive intention to motivate the child.

The infection of shame exacerbates the wounds of abandonment, and the pain grows. In the worst-case scenarios, such as sexual abuse or incest, toxic shame is a byproduct regardless of the messages a child received before the abuse occurred, or after it ended.

Contempt

In keeping with the analogy of a wound, *contempt is the scab* that forms over the infection of shame and the wound of abandonment [see Fig. 4]. The scab of contempt consists of all the "crusty" feelings of anger, resentment, and bitterness. It is what the child is most aware of, and it skews his whole experience of life as well as his role in it. Some call it the "life sucks" syndrome. The negative energy from the contempt must be directed somewhere. There are two possible choices, and the choice is made at an unconscious level. The energy can be directed inward in the form of self-contempt; or outward as contempt for people, society, authority figures, the opposite sex, or whoever is available, including God.

If we have a tendency to point the contempt inward at self, we are *internalizing* it. If we are more likely to turn it outward toward others, we are *externalizing* the contempt. The self-talk of an Internalizer is all about the defectiveness of self and his or her unworthiness to exist, leading to inappropriate guilt, and more shame, making the emotional infection worse. The self-talk of the Externalizer is all about the defectiveness of others and the unfairness of it all, leading to inappropriate anger.

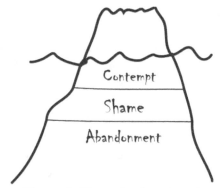

Figure 4: The scab of contempt

Many of us will internalize the contempt until we can't take it anymore and then blow up, directing it outward in an attempt to ventilate. When we externalize or "dump" our contempt it lands on whoever is nearby, usually those who are closest to us. Then, because we have hurt someone we love, we turn the contempt back on ourselves through more shame-based messages such as, *"See there. I've done it again ... I've hurt someone I care about! I've proven it this time ... I really am a loser!"* Internalizing the contempt feeds the infection of shame, speeding up its progression and the power it has over us.

Some people tend to internalize their contempt while others tend to externalize it. People who are primarily Internalizers have problems with depression, caretaking, approval-seeking, lack of adequate boundaries, and lack of a sense of personal power. They have difficulty saying, "no" because that may bring disapproval, which is extremely anxiety-provoking since it is the opposite of what they seek. Persons that are predominantly Externalizers are less likely to be aware of their behavior and the effect it has on others. They believe other people should do things their way, tend to be self-centered, intrusive, have rigid boundaries, may have an excessive need to be right, and proclaim that they don't need anyone.

Externalizers have a tendency to demonstrate what Bradshaw calls *"shameless behavior."* Shameless behavior is seen in situations of abuse where the abuser is exercising god-like control over the victim. Examples of shameless behavior include sexual, physical, and emotional abuse. Shameless Externalizers develop a very thick scab. In the extreme cases, the person involved in shameless behavior is unaware on a conscious level that his behavior is wrong or sometimes even that it is hurtful to the victim. On an unconscious level, Externalizers cannot escape the reality of their behavior or its impact on the victim. The unconscious mind knows all; the shame, guilt, and remorse continue to accumulate for Externalizers, even though they are largely unaware of it. As their infection of shame grows, so does their contempt along with the need to externalize it. This build-up of contempt may eventually lead the Externalizer to episodes of the violent and/or dangerous behavior described earlier in this chapter.

The False Self

The wound of abandonment, the infection of shame, and the scab of contempt forms a free-floating mass of pain just beneath the surface of our awareness which creates in a child a false sense of identity – A False Self [see Fig. 5].

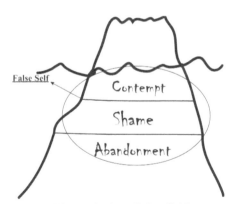

Figure 5: The False Self

The term "False Self" is used because it is just that—false, not true; a counterfeit self. It really feels like who we are, whether we were the child back there-and-then or the adult reading this book here-and-now. But this is not who we really are, and I hope to prove that in a moment. It *feels that way* because the wound is *emotional in nature.* Despite our best efforts, we cannot simply transfer the intellectual reality of this truth to our emotional reality. It is not until significant healing of the emotional wounds takes place that we are able to *feel* differently about ourselves.

Many times we have heard the saying, "kids are resilient." This is likely an effort to minimize our own guilt about not having been able to protect and/or nurture them the way they needed. While it is true that kids are resilient, the implication that they are now fine and have bounced back is not accurate. Emotional wounds do not go away. They must be tended to just like any other wound or the infection grows, and it gets worse. "Kids are survivors" is a more accurate statement. In the next chapter, we begin to explore how a child learns to survive and even get some of her needs met despite difficult circumstances. The skills they learn help them to survive, but they don't go very far in helping them effectively cope with adult life or have an intimate relationship.

Again, if you are a parent, please stay with your feelings about your own childhood experiences as much as possible as you read. Try to avoid getting lost in worry or guilt over your children. There is good news to come. For now, keep in mind that the best way to help them is to help *you* first. They learn by watching what you do, so demonstrate for them how to heal. Yes, get them into counseling if they need it and pay attention to their behavior if they are acting out. However, take care of yourself in the process too.

Chapter 3

The Art of Survival

In order for children to survive the pain of their wounds they must learn to live outside themselves; i.e., they must develop an *external focus* [see Fig. 6]. In other words, the child must find distractions in their outer world to avoid the pain of their inner world. Everything outside of our own skin is our outer world, while our thoughts and feelings exist only in our inner world. We experience our feelings in our body while our thoughts are located in our mind.

External Focus

Children develop this external focus through a number of distractions such as imaginary friends, relationships with pets or stuffed animals, watching cartoons, and staying busy with play. Later the distraction may be video games, skateboarding, or sports. Kids who have a lot of pain have difficulty with inactivity and quite time. One will often hear them proclaim, *"I'm bored! I can't stand boredom!"*

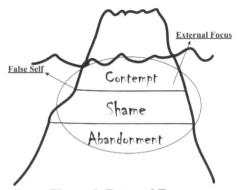

Figure 6: External Focus

In my work with teenagers, I encountered the "I can't stand boredom" syndrome many times before I learned that it really is true for some. Many kids have trouble tolerating boredom not because of boredom itself, but because of what boredom represents to them. Boredom to these wounded kids is a red flag. It's a signal that they are losing their external focus. As their attention begins to drift inward, anxiety starts to build because the next thing to come into their awareness would be their emotional pain. It rarely gets that far because the children or teenagers are compelled to take action to help them regain their external focus. A common scenario follows:

Billy, a teenager, is referred to counseling for habitually skipping school. Through the counseling process, it is discovered that this child's father is alcoholic and that things at home are fairly chaotic most of the time. In order to keep an external focus and avoid his emotional pain, Billy has to remain actively involved and interested in class. However, every day, right after lunch Billy has a math class. He is not interested in math at all because he is not very good at it (competence issue) so it is only a short time before "boredom" sets in.

Billy tries to regain his external focus by staring out the window in a daydream. That works for about three minutes. Soon, he finds himself passing notes, shooting spitballs, or talking to his neighbor. Before long, the teacher is involved in disciplining Billy, again, for disrupting the classroom. Billy then gets into an argument with his teacher, who is "always picking on me" (externalization of contempt). The teacher takes him out into the hall where the next external focus, the principal, is approaching.

Billy has the option of going through this routine or avoiding it altogether by skipping the class. The easiest option is to skip class and find some way to regain his external focus. Sometimes he would get a friend to sneak off with him to go to hangout downtown, or he would sneak off onto the parking lot to drink or do drugs, or simply go home to watch videos, play on the Internet, or engage in some other distraction.

Acting-out is only one method that helps children distract from their emotional pain. Again, other methods include creating imaginary friends, having relationships with stuffed animals or pets, video games, comic books, cartoons, hyperactivity, and various other ways to stay outside of themselves.

Invented Self

Another thing a child must do in order to avoid her inner world and stay in her outer world is to unconsciously build a wall between her awareness and her unawareness. These "walls" are constructed automatically of psychological defense mechanisms and have been collectively referred to as *"survival roles"* because their function is to help children survive in the face of unmet dependency needs. Children learn to "cover up" their false selves by projecting an image other people might find acceptable. This is often referred to as "wearing a mask." I think of it as inventing a self [see Fig. 7] to cover up the false self because, "If people really knew me they would not like me (shame), and they would reject me (fear of more abandonment)."

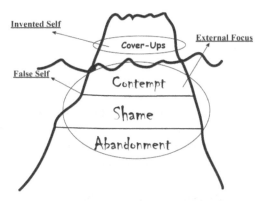

Figure 7: Invented Self

Children unwittingly invent and project these images, or survival roles, through the use of unconscious defense mechanisms in order to avoid the intolerable reality of their unmet needs. The pain is still there, but it is not as "in their face" as it would be due to one defense known as repression. Repression automatically pushes the pain deep into their subconscious until the child matures, and heals, enough to develop the psychological equipment to cope with it.

Survival roles also serve to help the child find ways to get her needs for time, attention, affection, and direction met. For example, in a dysfunctional family one parent gets caught up in some form of problematic behavior while the other gets caught up with trying to control or "fix" the problem parent. They get enmeshed with each other and the problem behavior while leaving less and less time to attend to anything else, including the children.

Family Hero:

When the first child comes along, he or she finds out fairly quickly that in order to get any time, attention, affection, and direction in this family he or she has to do something outstanding to get noticed. So this child usually becomes the *Hero*. There are two kinds of family heroes. The first is the flashy hero who gets all A's, is captain of the football team, valedictorian, class president, head cheerleader or a combination of the above. The second type is the behind-the-scenes hero; aka the *Responsible One* or the

Parentified Child. This is the child who comes home from school early every day, does the laundry, gets the mail, prepares dinner, does the dishes, takes care of the younger kids and, in essence, becomes a parent at ten years old.

Rebel/Scapegoat:

The second child usually becomes the *Rebel* or *Scapegoat*. They can rarely compete with the first child for the positive attention because the Hero has a head start. So the Rebel must settle for the next-best thing, i.e., negative attention. The Rebel gets time, attention, affection, and direction from teachers, principals, juvenile officers, counselors and anyone else who would try to help them. While they may not get the positive attention, they do end up getting the most attention. The parents must stop what they are doing to deal with this kid's misbehavior because the school or juvenile office keeps calling.

Lost Child:

The third child cannot compete for the positive attention or the negative attention, so they don't get any attention and become the *Lost Child*. In order to survive, this child relies on fantasy to get her needs partially met. An example of a Lost Child is the seven-year-old girl who is always somewhere in the background playing with a doll that she has had forever. One hardly ever notices she is even there. She says nice things to the doll, combs its hair, tucks it in every night, rocks it to sleep and, in essence, creates a family of her own, vicariously getting her needs met by becoming a nurturing parent to the doll. The Lost Child may also have anywhere from eight to twelve stuffed animals on her bed at one time and knows each of them intimately. This child spends so much time in her fantasy world that she loses out on opportunities to make friends in the real world.

Family Mascot:

The fourth child, usually the *Mascot*, is the baby of the family. This child gets his needs met through being on stage. He or she is the class clown or the beauty queen. This child's job is to entertain the family, usually in the form of humor.

The roles above are the classic survival roles described by Sharon Wegscheider-Cruse (1991) in her book *The Family Trap*. These roles do not always follow the pattern described above, but considerably more often than not, they do. The firstborn is usually the Hero because it is the preferred role, and the child has the first crack at it. All kids want the positive attention and honor assigned to the Hero. However, if that mask is taken, then the next children have to settle for the next-best thing. The Rebel is the second most effective role. Even though the attention is negative, they get lots more of it because the parents have to deal with this child's misbehavior, so the Rebel becomes the priority. Middle children are more like to get lost in the crowd, so they must sharpen their skills with fantasy in order to survive. These children also tend to be chameleons, switching from one survival role to another whenever the opportunity presents itself. Many times they experience all the roles in their life at one time or another. The baby of the family is almost always the center of attention so it is not surprising that these children make the most of that and become the Mascot.

So, it is *birth order*, not *personality*, not *willfulness*, and *not inherently bad character* that reinforces or "shapes" the original masks we learn to wear. Children do not decide to behave this way; they instinctively act-out these roles until they find the one that works the best in getting them the time, attention, affection and direction they need. Heroes get it from teachers, coaches, newspaper reporters, and others who are amazed by their outstanding abilities. Rebels gets it from teachers, principals, juvenile officers, counselors, and anyone else who wants to help them get back on track. The Lost Child gets it through fantasy, and the Mascot gets it through being on stage.

These roles are also reinforced at home because they all bring something to the family, helping the system to survive as well. The Hero brings honor to the family. The Rebel brings distraction, which takes the focus off the primary dysfunction in the marital pair. This is why another term used for the Rebel is "Scapegoat." They act as a lightning rod help to keep the family intact because, if the parents have too much time to face what is going on between them, they might get a divorce, and the family then disintegrates. The Lost Child brings relief because you never have to worry about this child and hardly notice he is there. The Mascot brings entertainment and humor, diffusing the seriousness of the family dysfunction. All of these roles look different on the outside, but they are all alike on the inside.

Impression Management

Another function of the Invented Self is to manage the impressions of others that are important to us. Impression Management is driven by the "what-would-other-people-think" syndrome. It goes something like this: If I have ten people in my life who are important to me, and one of them is not happy with me while the other nine think I am the greatest thing in the world, I would focus much of my energy thinking about how I could get that one back in line with the others. If two or three get upset with me, I get anxious. If four or five of them don't think much of me, I become desperate or panicky because it almost feels like I am dying.

It feels like I am dying because, in a way, I am. I draw my identity, my sense of self, from those ten people. Hen Hence, I must be vigilant in managing the impressions of those around me. If they accept me and think I am okay then I must be … right? Not necessarily—even if they accept me—I cannot truly accept their acceptance because, at another level, I feel like a phony. An example of this is when we have difficulty accepting compliments from others. Somewhere inside the voice of shame is telling us *"They wouldn't say that if they really knew you!"* The voice may even be inaudible, but we feel like a phony anyway. This accounts for the paradox of why we tend to discount or minimize anything positive coming from those we try to please.

The survival roles described above are examples of the masks we learn to wear in childhood. As we grow and the pain continues to accumulate, we get more and more sophisticated in the masks we wear. For a fairly complete catalog of masks, read John Powell's book (1995) *Why I am afraid to tell you who I am.*

Chapter 4

Who Am I Really?

As we have seen, the *False Self* is just that–false. It is an emotional wound and, like any other wound, it has gotten infected due to lack of attention. The severity of the wound of abandonment and the infection of shame are hard to see because they are covered by the scab of contempt, and for the most part, that wound is outside our awareness. We have also seen that our *Invented Self* is not who we are either. The False Self poses as our private self and the Invented Self as our public self, but both are imposters or counterfeits–so who are we really? For anyone who has ever struggled with addiction, codependency, and/or dysfunctional relationships, that is the million-dollar question.

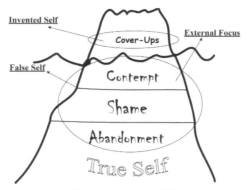

Figure 8: True Self

I mentioned in Chapter 2 that I think I can prove to the reader that the False Self is not who we really are. I know I can prove it to some, and I think I can prove it to others, but I am not sure I can prove it to all. Here goes: If you believe there is a Divine Creator, do you think He would want a small child to feel defective at her very core? Would a loving God want children to go through their entire childhood feeling rotten through and through? That everything bad that happens is their fault? Of course not!

This is proof *for believers* that the False Self is *not* what God created. No, these emotional wounds *are what life created*. The *True Self* is what God created, and it has been with us in our inner world since before we were born. Then life happened. The wounds grew and covered up the True Self, pushing it far beneath the surface of our awareness before we even had a chance to get to know ourselves. It was replaced with an imposter; as a child we bought it and learned to live outside ourselves, abandoning our inner world. Then we poured a slab of concrete over it (Invented Self), locking it all in place and effectively alienating ourselves from who we were created to be [Fig. 8].

It is my belief that the True Self is who God created and that this is where our spirit resides. I also believe this is why God feels especially far away to some. Our spirit is what connects with His Spirit. To the extent that we don't have access to our spirit, we feel cut off from God. Our True Self is also where our purpose resides. In Rick Warren's book, *A Purpose-Driven Life* (2002, 2007), the author points out that our purpose is not really *our* purpose at all … it is *His* purpose for us. We were created with a special set of talents and abilities in order to perform His purpose for us.

In the Bible, it says that *"He that is slow to anger is better than the mighty; and he that rules his spirit than he that takes a city."(KJV Prov. 16:32)* Do you wonder which "self" we are to overcome? In another place, the Bible says, *"Blessed are they that mourn: for they shall be comforted."* (KJV Matt. 5:4) Is *refusing to mourn* not what we do when we wear a mask, ignore our inner world, and pretend that everything is fine? When God feels far away, could it be because our True Self, the part of us that connects with /Him, is buried so deep under the wounds of the

WWW.INTERNET-OF-THE-MIND.COM

False Self that we cannot feel his presence? If the answers to these questions are "yes," then turning our focus inward to surface and grieve our pain is the royal road to *true comfort and relief.* As we shall see in the next chapter, seeking comfort and relief in all the wrong places inevitably leads to more pain.

Even if you are agnostic, or atheist, for that matter, I think most can believe in the innocence of a child. We all come into this world with a clean slate. Our true self gets wounded and covered up by this world regardless of our religious or spiritual beliefs. For those of you who believe neither in God, nor in the inherent goodness of man, I may not have been able to provide sufficient proof of the True Self. If not, I challenge you to look within and see if it might be contempt and emotional wounds that are getting in your way. I believe in you and wish you all the wonderful things that life has to offer.

The next logical questions are, *"How do we deal with this? How do we uncover our True Self?"* The good news is that there are answers to these questions. The bad news is that we first have more pain and consequences of emotional trauma to explore before we can answer them.

Chapter 5

Illusions of Comfort and Relief

Pain as a Motivator

As already pointed out, the role of pain in our life is to motivate us to do something different. Pain lets us know that what we are doing is not working by signaling that we are moving further away from happiness. It is a warning system that tells us when something is wrong or when something needs attention. Remember the formula from Chapter 1: A → B? This formula is not rocket science, so why do we keep doing the same things over and over expecting a different outcome each time? The easiest answer to that question is *because we don't know what else to do*. We are all doing our best to achieve that one ultimate goal in life: to be happy. Perhaps happiness eludes us due to the progressively dysfunctional methods we unwittingly rely upon to feel better. Soon the best we can hope for is comfort and relief.

We don't like pain and when we encounter it, we are compelled to seek comfort and relief. Growing up with all of this woundedness is painful. So where do we find comfort and relief? We cannot generate any good feelings on the inside because we can't even go there, it is too painful. So, we must look to things outside of ourselves for comfort and relief. Since we are all genetically and psychologically "wired" a little differently, we will find one or two things that "really does it" for us. Some of us are wired for alcohol or other drugs, others for excessive working, spending, drama, risk-taking, sexing, gambling, eating, and others for addictive relationships. These are only a few of the distractions available to us in this candy store we call America [Fig. 9]

Emotional Attachments

When we find the object or event that "really does it for us" then we attach to it on an emotional level because *we love what it does for us*. It provides us with a very powerful, instantaneous, although short-lived, feeling. Soon *we begin to trust the object or event* because it does what it is supposed to do (make us feel better) very quickly, very powerfully, and in a way no one and nothing else can − every single time we ask it to. So, we attach to the object or event on an emotional level.

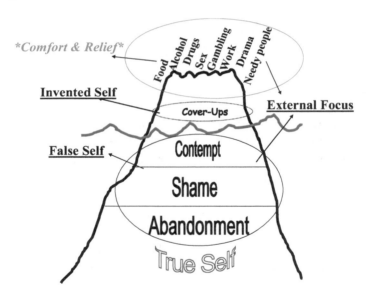

Figure 9: Comfort and Relief

Love and trust are the main ingredients for a primary relationship. This emotional attachment signals the beginning of a serious problem because we are not supposed to have primary relationships with objects and events. Our primary relationships are supposed to be with people who are important to us. Craig Nakken defines addiction in his book, *The Addictive Personality.* According to Nakken, addiction is "a pathological relationship with an object or event that produces a desired mood swing." This is, in my opinion, the best definition of addiction I have heard. I do, however, take the liberty of making one minor distinction for the benefit of my clients. I define addiction as *"an unhealthy primary relationship with an object or event that produces a desired mood swing."* I make this distinction for a couple of reasons. First of all, "pathological" seems to produce more stigma than "unhealthy" even though they mean the same thing. Secondly, "primary" highlights why the relationship is unhealthy.

Most people don't realize and will, in fact, initially deny that they have such a strong emotional attachment to their addiction of choice. In both treatment groups and individual sessions, I have asked my addicted clients the following question for the past several years, always with the same results: *"What is the most important relationship in your life?"* They will respond with *"My wife, my kids, my mom, my boyfriend or girlfriend."* I always just shake my head and say *"Wrong answer."* They initially get a little indignant that I would be so presumptuous to assume I know what is more important to them than they do themselves. Then all I have to say is *"When was the last time you lied to your mom about ..., broke a promise to your kids about ..., broke up with a girlfriend over...."* etc. There is rarely an argument. I close this discussion with *"Maybe in your heart, they are most important to you, but in your life the reality is addiction trumps everything else."*

Let's look for a moment at the implications of this emotional attachment to an object or event. First of all, the question of "choice" frequently comes up. For example, "He chose to start; he can choose to stop!" This attachment is a love and trust relationship just like any other love and trust relationship. When was the last time you "chose" to fall in love with someone? How easy is it to end a relationship with someone you love, even when you know it is for the best? When you do end such a relationship you can expect to grieve. Since this is one of the most important relationships in your life the grief process kicks in full-steam when one decides to get help and give up your addiction. This is manageable if we have the internal coping skills and external support network to manage the pain of this "letting-go" process. However, if we have this unhealthy primary relationship in the first place, that implies that we have neither the skills nor the support necessary to manage the pain associated with this loss. So we fall back on the object or activity that we trust the most. This is precisely why people relapse into their addiction and precisely how they eventually lose their "choice" to "just quit." To make matters worse, in some cases, there is the physical pain of withdrawal to contend with as well.

The comfort we achieve through this relationship with an object or event is an illusion. Remember, the wounds we must heal in order to be happy is *emotional in nature*. Therefore, we need emotional comfort and relief, such as the kind we get when our basic needs are met, in order to heal and be healthy. The "comfort and relief" we achieve through the use of our object or event of choice is not emotional but physiological, or physical, in nature. In other words, we learn to mask our emotional pain with "medicine." That means any time we have a feeling we don't like, we medicate it rather than listen to it, understand it, and respond to it. This just pushes the feeling back down inside to accumulate with the pain that is already there. Using a chemical to medicate our emotional pain is tantamount to masking a serious back injury with painkillers while we go on working. We keep doing more and more damage without realizing it because our "warning system" (pain) was taken out of the way. Thus we continue to do things to increase our shame, guilt, contempt, and remorse. We prove it over and over again, that "we can't do anything right." We eventually abandon our money, our families, our cars, our pride, our careers, our dreams, our goals, ourselves, etc. As our pain increases, so does our need for "comfort and relief" [Fig. 9].

Sooner or later we will crash and "hit bottom" [Fig. 10]. This happens when we have accumulated so much pain that there is not enough "comfort and relief" to offset it anymore. The "coping skill" that used to work instantly now only barely works. This is when we are using our addiction just to feel normal. Some addictions get us there faster than others. Some addictions are too easy to hide. For instance, if we are addicted to alcohol, we can get a DWI or DUI, but if we have an addiction to work, we get a bonus.

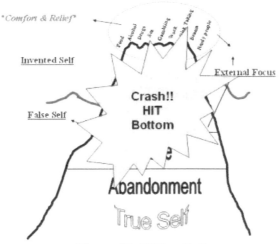

Figure 10: Hitting Bottom

Hitting Bottom

A major obstacle to hitting bottom is well-intentioned others who enable us by interfering with the A → B formula mentioned earlier. People who love and care about us want to help when we are in trouble. For example, when we do "A" (spend our rent money on alcohol) we should receive "B" (have to deal with it ourselves–i.e., take on extra work to pay the rent or be evicted). However, when someone steps in and gives us "C" (pays our rent for us "this time") instead of letting us experience "B," that person has become our enabler. "Enablers" help maintain our addiction a little longer by reducing or eliminating our pain. Remember, pain is a motivator and teacher. "Tough Love" means stepping out of the way and letting us experience "B." Often times our chief enabler is just as wounded as we are, so we have become his external focus. Think about it, what better way to distract from our own problems than to find a "problem person" to focus on. We tend to choose people on an unconscious, as well as a conscious, level. This explains how many people end up getting out of one bad relationship only to find that they are right back in another. Such people have an excessive need to be needed. They are Internalizers who find comfort and relief by becoming important to others. You will often hear other people say about them, *"What a saint of a woman! Look at all she goes through, and still she sticks with him!"* The masks they wear include the Martyr, The Rescuer, and the Victim.

Until we get our wake-up call, unconscious psychological defenses block acceptance of the reality and extent of our addiction. Examples are: *Rationalization* (Excuse-making, justifying); *Projection* (Blaming anything and anyone except the real problem); *Minimizing* (It's not that bad, I can quit anytime I want); *Diversion Tactics* (Debating, arguing, withdrawing, and changing the subject); *Disarming* (That's just the way I am), *Hostility* (Intimidating others who try to talk about it); etc.

When the "call" does come, we are likely to reach out for help. The irony of this is that many people who reach out for help with their pain don't really want to know what's bothering them because their denial is still intact. They just know they want comfort and relief. For those readers who need help, I hope this book will raise your bottom level to the point you get it sooner than later. Unfortunately, some have a very high tolerance for pain, and they wait too long and some tragedy strikes. You don't have to wait until that happens. It is not easy, but with honesty, open-mindedness, and willingness you can recover!

Chapter 6

The Twilight Zone

Recovery from addiction is easy–*all you have to do is change your whole life*.

The transition from the old life to the new is a period of limbo where the past is too painful to return and the future is too uncertain to feel comfortable about. There is much to be done, and it cannot be done all at once. If people plunge headlong into their emotional pain, they will be compelled to seek comfort and relief in the only way they know how, which results in a relapse into their addiction of choice. The first thing one must do is give up his comfort and relief [Fig. 12], accept that he cannot recover alone, and reach out to others for help. For these reasons, the *pain of not reaching out* for help must outweigh the *pain of continuing to engage* in the addiction.

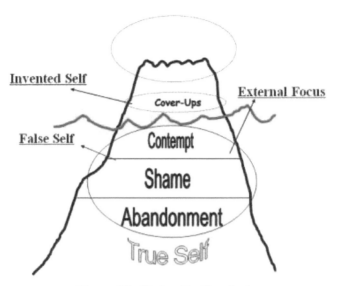

Figure 12: Giving Up Comfort

Reaching Out

Reaching out to others is an interpersonal skill that we are not born with. *Acting out* is the instinct children are born with in order to express their needs. If we grew up with a significant amount of emotional pain, then we are not likely to be very good at reaching out because it was either not taught or not allowed. Furthermore, the infection of shame makes it very difficult to ask for help. Often, it is only when the pain grows to an unbearable proportion that we begin to consider reaching out. Adding the accumulated shame of our entire life with having to admit a problem with alcohol, drugs, sex, food, or gambling, to name a few, gives us an idea of the magnitude of the problem one can have with asking for help. Can you hear the voice of shame? *"See, now you are really proving what a loser you are!"*

Reaching out requires a certain amount of self-disclosure; i.e., taking off the mask of the Invented-Self. The need to manage the impressions of others cries out to keep quiet and find some other way to work this out. This is the primary reason that such value is placed upon the anonymity of members of 12-Step groups. They realize the importance of safety to those newcomers who may be considering reaching out for help by attending a meeting for the first time. Even when the pain is great enough to bring someone in for counseling, they are compelled to manage the impression of the counselor to the extent that it can actually sabotage the assessment process. Here people who have "reached out" by making the counseling appointment will answer many of the questions in a way that suggests they are fine and there really is no problem. Sometimes it takes a few sessions before they begin to feel safe enough with the helper, the environment, and the confidentiality to open up.

Internalizers are a little more likely to reach out early than Externalizers because the latter have an excessive need to be right. Externalizers are "shameless" because their defenses are geared toward making everyone else responsible for their problems. To admit a problem of any kind requires taking an inward look. This is highly irregular for an Externalizer because her shamelessness is in proportion to the actual shame and pain she would feel if she could see the truth. So, again, the pain of hitting bottom must outweigh the pain of facing her inner world before she is motivated to reach out.

On the other hand, the defenses of Internalizers are geared toward self-contempt. They are "not important, never right about anything, total failures, and unworthy of happiness." These are the very depressing thoughts of an Internalizer which make him depressed even before the wake-up call comes. Again, most people are rarely at one end of the contempt continuum or the other, although there are some cases in which this is true. More often, we have a tendency to slide up and down on that line internalizing for as long as we can stand it then blowing up occasionally to externalize, or dump, some of that contempt.

When people do feel enough pain to come in for help, many times their denial is still largely intact. They may say, "I am here to get help with my depression." The therapist might ask, "Why are you depressed?" Client: "I don't know." Therapist: "Well, do you drink?" Client: "Yes, but that's not my concern right now." Therapist: "How much and how often do you drink?" Client, "Probably too much, I have had three DUIs, but that's not why I am here. I came because I am depressed." Therapist: "If that is not the problem then do you have any theories about what is?" Client, "You're the therapist, you tell me!"

This person is still looking for ways to avoid giving up his unhealthy primary relationship with alcohol. He wants help to find comfort and relief but is still fighting that painful inward look. He is already in pain and to let go of his denial too soon might be overwhelming. Care must be taken to go forward at an acceptable pace, building coping skills and supports first. If one is to give up their primary coping skill, he must have something to replace it prior to doing the work ahead. Even then, the pain gets worse before it gets better.

People who reach out later than sooner are usually so full of shame that, when they do take that initial inward look, they say things like, *"Man, I don't even have any values anymore!"* I had one person tell me they felt that they had actually become evil. In addition to the toxic shame, what they have become emotionally infected with is the normal guilt and remorse they feel for the bad things they have done during their addiction. The food addict is full of shame over repeated failures to control eating. The sex addict is full of shame over the inability to honor the marriage by staying faithful. The gambling addict is full of shame over the inability to take care of his family due to overwhelming debt. The work-a-holic is full of shame over hundreds of broken promises to spend time with his wife and kids.

Recovery – A Hard Sell

Imagine you are reaching out for help because you are in the most emotional pain you have ever felt. Now imagine hearing the helper say that you need to give up the only comfort and relief you've ever known and face this pain [Fig. 12]. That's what it is like for someone who finds himself at the bottom. It is a very hard sell even when the person knows you are right. Along with reaching out, abstinence is another of the first things we need to accomplish if we are going to heal.

At this point, some simple definitions are in order. *Abstinence* means not engaging in *any* unhealthy relationships with objects or events to produce a desired mood swing. Many times people give up their addiction of choice only to begin relying on another unhealthy relationship to medicate their pain. Alcoholics may switch to marijuana; sex addicts may switch to gambling, gambling addicts to drinking, compulsive spenders to food, etc. This is called *substitution* because we are simply substituting *one unhealthy relationship for another*. It's like a rebound relationship; how long are we likely to stay with our second choice when we know our first choice is waiting in the wings? This is a strategy many people employ even before they get to the point of needing to reach out. It doesn't work because it only addresses the need for comfort and relief. The rest of The Iceberg remains intact. Sooner or later the emotional pain flares up again and the substitute just doesn't get it. *Cross-addiction* is what happens when the substitute *does just as much* for us as the unhealthy relationship of choice. But now we have two addictions to overcome, because the new one almost always leads back to the old one.

Abstinence is a required task in order for recovery to take place. How does one abstain from food addictions, sex addiction, work addictions, and spending addictions? Abstinence in these cases means using the objects and events only in the healthy ways for which they are intended. This means we eat for the right reasons, we have sex for the right reasons with the right person, we balance work with the other areas of our lives, and we spend money for the right reasons. We avoid self-medicating while improving emotional coping skills, building a support network, learning how to communicate, and healing the internal wounds.

Prescription for Recovery

Recovery means abstaining and liking it better than engaging in unhealthy relationships with objects or events. The only time we are going to like abstinence better than engaging in our addictions is when we find comfort from the internal healing that begins to take place. This healing can only occur through the development of healthy recovery-oriented behaviors and activities.

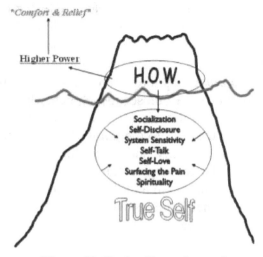

Figure 13: Turing Focus Inward

In the 12-Step groups, suggested recovery activities are:
- Go to Recovery Meetings
- Get a Sponsor
- Pray and Meditate
- Read Recovery Literature
- Practice the 12 Steps of Recovery

In his Video *Shame and Addiction* John Bradshaw suggests:
- Socialization – Attend non-shaming recovery or church groups
- Self-Disclosure – Come out of hiding, break the no-talk rule
- System Sensitivity – Understand the family system you came from
- Self-Talk – Positive affirmations
- Self-Love – Take care of yourself
- Surfacing the Pain – Talk about it, understand it, get it out
- Spirituality – Prayer and Meditation

Relapse means undoing recovery enough to be able to return to an unhealthy relationship. Relapse is a process that ends when we re-engage our addictive relationship of choice. One cannot relapse without a period of recovery. A period of abstinence with no recovery activities is called *stopping*. Stopping is easy; staying stopped is the hard part. Stopping is always followed by starting again. This is why a good friend of mine in recovery likes to say, *"I can't stop drinking because if I stop, I know I will start again."* He reminds himself and others, "I can abstain one day at a time by the grace of a power greater than myself."

What Next?

As mentioned throughout this book, arresting addictions, codependency, chronic depression, and other long-term life problems is a critical piece of recovery, but it is only the *tip of the Iceberg*. Stabilizing these conditions through the development of healthy coping skills and a good support network is the foundation for the work that lies ahead. Many people recover through the use of 12-Step programs and other community support programs alone. Some people speed up the healing process with the inclusion of therapy as part of their recovery program. However, what about that one ultimate goal that we all have in common—that state of being that we all pursue so vigorously? I have found that happiness–i.e., *contentment, fulfillment, satisfaction, wholeness and completeness*–is not something we can seek and find. It is a byproduct of living the way we were intended to live—as our True Self [Fig. 14]. Codependency, chronic depression, Adult/Child Syndrome, and the many other long-term consequences of abandonment, shame and contempt are OPTIONAL. You don't have to live that way anymore. If you feel ready now, begin working on Part I of the *Thawing the Iceberg* recovery program in the following pages.

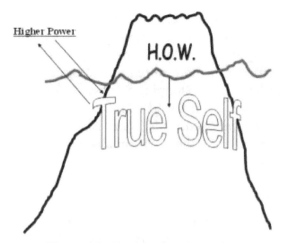

Figure 14: Finding Your True Self

Thawing
Toxic Relationships

The Workbook

Introduction:

Carl Jung once said, *"You cannot have another relationship until you first finish your source relationships."* This statement implies that you can have as many relationships as you want, but they will follow the same pattern as those original relationships of your family of origin. Therefore, if you want a *different kind* of relationship, you must first finish the unfinished business in those original or "source" relationships.

It has also been said many times, in many ways, *"You cannot have a good relationship with others until you first develop a good relationship with yourself."* How does one have a relationship with oneself? *Thawing Adult/Child Syndrome* answered that question in that it focused on *intra-personal* dynamic; i.e., the functioning of various ego-states also known as aspects or parts of the whole personality.

It is assumed that the reader has completed the *Thawing Adult/Child Syndrome* workbook and, having gained adequate self-awareness and inner harmony between parts, is now prepared to begin working on *interpersonal* dynamics; i.e., your relationships with others. In a sense, we are going to look at and improve "how your parts play with their parts."

Separateness & Connectedness

The focus of this work being interpersonal relationships, it is important to introduce a central principle of interpersonal functioning—the dynamic interplay between one's ability to connect with another person, while maintaining enough separateness to maintain an autonomous sense of self.

Any therapist who does marital and relationship counseling will spend a lot of time assessing the separateness and connectedness of a couple who comes in for help. The ability to maintain a solid sense-of-self (separateness) is critical to being able to co-create a healthy relationship. Likewise, the ability to bond and share "who one really is" with another person (connectedness) is also a requirement for true intimacy.

To get an idea of a healthy separateness and connectedness, spread your fingers and bring both of your hands together touching only at the finger tips and thumbs. Here you see two parts creating one whole (connectedness). However, you can also see where one part begins and the other ends because there is a healthy boundary between the two (separateness).

Growing up in a less-than-nurturing family usually impairs abilities for healthy separateness and connectedness which, as we shall see, is the foundation for most relationship problems. To get a sense of these problems, interlace your fingers as if you are folding your hands. This is all connectedness and no separateness. Two terms used in family therapy for this dysfunctional connection are *fusion* or *enmeshment*. The enmeshed couple has become so tangled up with each other emotionally that it's hard to tell where one ends and the other begins—they have lost their healthy boundary. Enmeshment may look equal but it is not. One person gets *swallowed-up,* or *engulfed,* by the other, losing their autonomy and sense-of-self. An Externalizer (see Section 1:1) usually does the swallowing and the Internalizer usually gets swallowed-up.

Now separate your hands by about six to eight inches. Here you can see all separateness and no connection. Family therapists call this a *disengaged* relationship style. The wide boundary between them is created and maintained by distancing behaviors such as physical absence, emotional withdrawal, retreating into an activity such as work, television, reading, or busyness. Extra-marital affairs, frequent bursts of rage or anger, and disappearing on an addictive binge for days and weeks at a time are the more severe forms of distancing behavior.

Distance and pursuit behaviors are programmed survival strategies used to control or regulate the safe-distance between each other in a dysfunctional relationship. As already mentioned, it is healthy to have some separateness in the relationship in order to preserve a sense-of-self. The healthy way to regulate that distance is to set healthy boundaries by saying, hearing, and accepting the word "no." In a dysfunctional family or relationship, saying and/or hearing the word "no" is usually a no-no. Externalizers (Distancers) have difficulty hearing and accepting the word "no" while Internalizers (Pursuers) generally have trouble saying the word "no" because *"If I say no you might leave me"*; fear of abandonment.

Distance, Pursuit, and Ego-State Functioning

From a Transactional Analysis (TA) perspective, impaired regulation of separateness is the function of the ***Angry/Defiant Child*** ego-state while impaired regulation of connectedness is the function of the ***Vulnerable/Needy Child*** ego-state. The Vulnerable/Needy Child ego-state develops in the earliest years of life when experiences in our parental relationships impact the development of our ability to trust, nurture, and connect with self and others. This is the time in life when we are the most vulnerable and defenseless.

We need the energy of the Vulnerable/Needy ego-state in order ***to connect with others***, *as well as ourselves*. If our family is healthy and provides a "safe container" in which to grow and develop, then our ability to be vulnerable and connect with others is likely to be whole and intact. On the other hand, if we are not protected in the safe container of a healthy family then we are exposed to experiences that create the original wounds of abandonment—our abilities to connect are then impaired by fear of abandonment and/or fear of intimacy.

We need the Angry/Defiant Child energy in order ***to separate from others*** *and maintain an independent sense-of-self*. This part

52

of us also begins to develop in the first years of life. Consider what is commonly referred to as the *Terrible Two's*—this is when the child makes his/her first bid for autonomy or separateness by saying the word "no." How that developmental task is tolerated and responded to by the parents will set the stage for the official debut of the Angry/Defiant Child ego-state at twelve to thirteen years old. Puberty is the onset of adolescence when separateness is the major theme.

It is through these and other developmental tasks of childhood and adolescence that the patterns for separateness and connectedness (or distance and pursuit) are set into place.

Journal Exercise – Take a moment to close your eyes, relax and review a chronological timeline; i.e., a history of your adult relationships. Now reread the above sections and answer as many of the following questions as you can.

1. What patterns do you see? With what parts of the reading do you most identify? Are you a distancer or pursuer? Do you more easily experience your Angry/Defiant energy or your Vulnerable/Needy energy in your adult relationships?

2. **Now go even further back in time:** What about your parents? Was one more distant and the other more needy and vulnerable? Were they disengaged or enmeshed? Did one of them seem to try to "engulf" you or ignore you as a child? Were you allowed to have your own feelings and opinions – was it Ok to be you, or did you feel pressure to be what they wanted you to be?

The Chemistry of Drama

Over the years I have taken a LOT of codependent relationship histories from people who came to counseling with "toxic" or addictive relationship problems. It almost never fails that when I ask "Was there ever anyone in your history who really treated you well, was a reliable, stable person and really cared about you?" The answer is usually something like, "Well, yes...there was this one person who was really great, seemed to really like me, and treated me really well." When I enquire as to what happened, the answer usually is something like, "I don't really know, we just fizzled-out," or "I guess we just didn't hit it off," or "We didn't seem to click," or "We just quit calling each other." In other words, there was NO CHEMISTRY in that relationship!

Throughout the remainder of this book we will frequently refer back to the cycle outlined below. I refer to this cycle as the **Chemistry of Drama.** It is this very bio-chemistry that puts the "toxicity" in a toxic relationship. Out of it springs all the dysfunctional patterns that are so predictable. The psychological and behavior cycles are fueled by this chemistry. This includes well-documented patterns such as the *Drama Triangle,* the *Punishment/Forgiveness Cycle,* the *Enabling Trap,* the *Figure Eight, Relationship Mind Games,* and the *Distance & Pursuit Game.* This common denominator is actually a cycle of biological changes in the mind-and-body that contains within it a "payoff" for playing these games. This *Chemistry of Drama* is the "hook" for addictive relationships.

The chemistry within the cycle outlined below is not something we think about or are even consciously aware of (until we see it in print like I am about to show you). Here is a brief description of the chemistry at the core of the many variations of codependent relationship patterns:

1. Things are okay and we are doing fine.

2. One or both of us gets a little bored with "fine" because there is no chemistry in that. So one of us says or does just the right thing, at just the wrong time, causing a fight or other drama.

3. During the fight our abandonment, shame, and contempt gets activated. We experience an escalating negative chemistry flowing through our system (adrenalin, cortisol, and other stress hormones) —just think of them as "little red frowns" flowing through our blood stream. As the drama progresses, we

feel increasingly NOT Ok due to our threats of abandonment, shaming one another, and/or spewing of contempt!

4. Toward the end of the drama we begin looking for ways to make up so we can "be OK" again as a couple—usually this is just a retreat, cease fire, and/or truce with nothing actually getting resolved.

5. Having "made up" with each other we are ""OK" again as a couple. At this point, we experience an internal sense of "being OK again" on the inside too. This is the positive chemistry that comes with comfort and relief —little yellow happy faces begin flowing through our system, (or at lease little grey strait faces) because dopamine and other natural morphine-like chemicals are released when a crisis is over.

6. However, this comfort and relief is only a temporary condition that soon fades away—leaving NO CHEMISTRY! But we are "doing fine" again, for a while.

7. In order to have more chemistry in our codependent relationship, one of us must instigate another round of this cycle. It is not that we want that negative side of the cycle, it is that we are conditioned to seek the positive chemistry of comfort and relief that comes with making up, so...*We MUST go through the negative part of the cycle in order to set-up the positive part of the cycle.*

8. Finally, in order to maintain this important cycle, denial must be present to prevent conscious awareness of it, lest we become obliged to give it up. So, unless we get rigorously honest with ourselves, we really believe our rationalizations, projections, and blaming of the other person as the guilty party when it is actually both of us dancing the only dance we know. (Thank goodness we can learn a new dance!)

In summary, it is the "comfort and relief" or "making-up" chemistry in the Cycle of Drama that provides the primary fuel for addiction. We cannot access the comfort and relief unless we first re-enact those familiar emotional themes of abandonment, shame, and/or contempt. There is also a secondary, somewhat brief but weirdly-satisfying, payoff that comes with the confirmation of our existential position outlined in *Thawing Adult/Child Syndrome.*

Furthermore, without the entire cycle, we would feel NO chemistry and therefore no reinforcing payoff without these distance and pursuit or other psychological mind games. This is most likely the reason we are NOT attracted to "normal," stable people who don't engage in drama.

Journal Exercise – Take a moment to explore and answer as many of the following questions as you can.

1. What patterns do you see in your relationship cycle? With what parts of the reading do you most identify? See if you can overlay your own specific patterns onto the general description above. Does "the shoe fit?" How?

2. **Now, go even further back in time:** What about your relationships with your parents? Do you see how they may have acted out this cycle in their own way with each other? Did you experience something like this Chemistry of Drama in a cycle of your own with one or both parents? Take some time to explore and write as much as you can about that as it will be useful as you continue reading.

Section 1: Core Issues

Erik Erikson outlines eight human development stages of life. These stages ultimately shape how we behave in relationships by influencing our core issues – i.e., personality traits, existential positions (*Ok - Not Ok*), ego-state functioning, and relationship styles.

1.1 Relationship Styles; Codependence & Counter-Dependence

Reading the Iceberg Model in the first chapters of this book (p. 21) and throughout *Thawing Adult/Child Syndrome*, you have undoubtedly seen multiple references to the terms *"Externalizer"* and *"Internalizer."* These two relationship styles are not something we are born with. They are molded and shaped by developmental processes and other experiences during childhood.

Internalizing Abandonment, Shame, and Contempt is the primary behavioral pattern of a **Codependent**; Externalizing is the primary behavioral pattern that fits with Gorski and Black's description of the **Counter-Dependent.** Both of these relationship styles exist on a continuum.

Externalizer		Internalizer
Counter-Dependent		Co-Dependent

If we grew up in a dysfunctional family we probably move up and down on this negative continuum, unless we get stuck at one end or the other. Moving back and forth or getting stuck on this continuum is not a good thing either way if we want to have healthy and fulfilling relationships – but, until we make necessary changes, this may be the best we can do because of inadequate training and a lack of experience in healthy intimacy.

The very nature and "chemistry" of our connectedness to our mother in the first stage of life, along with the permission given for us to separate in the second stage, sets the pace for how we connect and separate in later significant relationships. Will we develop a healthy balance of connectedness and separateness (Intimacy)? Or must we pursue an unavailable partner, driven by fear of abandonment (Codependent)? Or distance ourselves from such connections driven by a fear of being trapped (Counter-dependent)?

Each developmental stage will influence and reinforce the outcomes of the previous stage. When growing up in a less-than-nurturing-family system, many factors and significant emotional events occur during the course of human development stages that influence which relationship style is formed – I use the word "formed" vs. "chosen" because kids really have no conscious choice in such matters; even though, as we shall see later, they do make decisions about themselves, others, and life in general, without words, at a subconscious level (aka, the *Little Professor*). These decisions are referred to as **Psychological Positions**. The following is a brief review of these:

1.1.1 Psychological Positions

1. **I'm OK, You're OK** (healthy position) *"Life is worth living."*

This is potentially a mentally healthy position. If realistic, people with this position about themselves and others can solve their problems constructively. Their expectations are likely to be realistic. They accept the significance of other people and life in general. (*Adult and Healthy Parent ego-state chemistry; "doing fine," able to grow and self-actualize*)

2. **I'm OK, You're Not-OK** (Externalizer position) *"Your life is not worth much."*

This is the position of persons who feel victimized or persecuted, so they victimize and persecute others. They blame others for their miseries. In its worst form, troubled teens and adult criminals often have this position which in *extreme* cases may lead to homicide. (*Angry/Defiant Child and externalized Critical Parent chemistry; self-empowerment and contempt for others, "fight" response*)

3. **I'm Not-OK, You're OK** (Internalizer position) *"My life is not worth much."*

This is a common position of persons who feel powerless when they compare themselves to others. This position leads them to withdraw, to experience depression, and, in severe cases, to become suicidal. (*Vulnerable Child and internalized Critical Parent chemistry; shame and self-contempt, "flight" response*)

4. **I'm Not-OK, You're Not-OK** (futility position) *"Life itself isn't worth much."*

This is the position of those who lose interest in living, who experience a rapid cycling between all positions. In extreme cases, this position can also lead to suicide or homicide. (*Vulnerable Child, Angry/Defiant Child, AND Critical Parent chemistry; helplessness, hopelessness, and worthlessness, "freeze" response*)

When making decisions about themselves, children may conclude:

I'm OK	**I'm not OK**
I'm smart	I'm stupid
I'm empowered	I'm inadequate
I'm good enough	I'm no good
I'm confident	I'm bad, unworthy
I can reach my goals	I can't do anything

When making decisions about others, children may conclude:

People are Ok	**People are not OK**
People are generally giving	People are selfish
Men are Okay	Men are no good
People are helpful	People are don't care
I know people like me	Nobody likes me
People are good	People are evil

When making decisions about life, children may conclude:

Life is OK	**Life is not OK**
The world is safe	The world is dangerous
Life is good	Life sucks

As mentioned above, children don't choose these positions; they are formed or shaped by an ongoing, dynamic interplay between the child and forces in its environment; i.e., parents, authority figures, and the unique circumstances of the family. During the early, formative years, these positions are set up by "felt-thought" because there are no words or self-talk yet.

The first seven years are the frequently referred to as the "formative" years because this is when life-long attitudes, programming, and psychological positions begin to take "form." The first four pre-verbal years, when words and the ability to reason do not yet exist for the child, is the most formative time. The child's learning is shaped and formed primarily by stimulus-response conditioning (in short, the "chemistry" we discussed on pp. 58-60 above)

Sometime around seven years of age is when the words and self-talk come along. Up until then the child has only the feelings and bio-chemistry, but when they get the words it can be very powerful because the meaning of the feeling can suddenly become "known" to the child. For example, "Daddy drinks so much because I am such a bad kid!"

It is at this point that decisions are made about self, others, and the world in general. These decisions become the basis of the psychological positions already described. It is the chemistry of drama that locks in the position because during the negative side of the cycle there is that payoff of "confirmation of the psychological position." For example, during another episode of drunken behavior, he comes home and stumbles on a toy lying on the floor. He then grabs another beer and starts yelling at the child about leaving his toys out "all over the floor." The child gets that "feeling" (along with the chemistry) and experiences self-talk like this, "There you go again! You are so stupid! You should be ashamed of yourself! If it weren't for you he wouldn't be drinking so much!"

With repetition and intensity, the above experience reinforces the child's psychological positions about self, others, and/or the world in general. In this case, it may be something like this: "I am just no good!" "Other people's behavior is my responsibility," and "Life is always such a struggle!"

There may even be a payoff on the negative side of this cycle of drama. Take the "life is not ok" position (i.e., "Life is always such a struggle"), for example. At the first sign of problems someone with this position may get a weirdly satisfying sensation that goes with the self-statement: "I just knew it!! Nothing is ever easy!!" This is the Confirmation of the Existential or Psychological Position. That somewhat gratifying charge is likely to come from an illusion control that comes with having a good "grasp on reality." *"Ah Ha... I was right yet again!"*

Journal Exercise – Take a moment to explore and answer as many of the following questions as you can in your Journal.

1. With which of the above psychological positions do you most identify? Do you bounce between internalizing and externalizing? When are you most likely to do that? What are your triggers for each of those positions?

2. Can you identify a cycle of drama between your parents or caretakers? What usually set it in motion? Describe the pattern, how it felt to be you watching that cycle, and the self-talk that might have gone with all that.

3. Can you begin to identify a cycle and the Chemistry of Drama between you and your parent(s)? What usually set it in motion? Describe the pattern, how it felt to be you during the cycle, and the self-talk that might have gone with all that.

4. What are some of the decisions you made about yourself, others and the world in general from these experiences?

5. Can you see yourself re-enacting these patterns and emotional themes with your partners in adulthood?

1.2 Erikson's Eight Developmental Stages

According to Erikson, *each stage of development involves a crisis. It's the resolution of this crisis that determines the outcome of a specific stage; i.e., positive or negative.* Negative outcomes fall on a continuum between what I have referred to as Externalization and Internalization. Positive outcomes do not fall on a continuum as they represent a healthy adjustment to that stage.

All other things being equal, kids who consistently get appropriate parenting throughout these developmental stages are expected to have good outcomes as one stage builds on the outcome of the previous stage. But kids who do not get the parenting they need are expected to have deficits in various stages. School, church, and other influences may also have an impact on the outcomes.

As you review the stages outlined below, notice how one end of the negative outcomes continuum clearly describes the characteristics of *the Angry/Defiant Child* ego-state, while the other end clearly defines the characteristics of the *Vulnerable/Needy Child* ego-state. Those who have experienced negative outcomes – most of us to some degree – can slide up and down on that continuum according to the circumstances and situation. However, those who have been hurt the worst may have excluded or "disowned" one of those ego-states. As we learned in *Thawing Adult/Child Syndrome*, those who discount one portion of reality, in this case an ego-state, tend to magnify the other portion of reality (the opposite ego state) – giving the impression of being stuck on one end of the continuum.

Significantly negative outcomes result in the development of the full continuum. In other words, wounded people frequently hold two or more psychological positions at once. However, through the use of adaptive defenses employed by the *Little Professor,* one ego-state, holding one position, is experienced consciously; while the excluded or disowned ego-state, holding another position, is experienced at a subconscious or pre-conscious level and even "triggered" into conscious awareness when the situation or circumstances are right. But typically, only one ego-state can be active (aka, cathected) at a given time. Other ego-states can be aware, but only as observers who are not able to "drive the bus," so to speak.

Journal Exercise – Explore each of the following Stages of Development. Check off any items that apply to your adult life and relationships. Make notes about your thoughts and observations, especially those to which you strongly relate. You may even want to review the "Script Elements" in *Thawing Adult Child Syndrome* before completing this exercise. The goal is to identify your core developmental issues.

NOTE: If you have completed *Thawing Childhood Abandonment Issues* you will have a lot of this information already. If you have not completed *Thawing Childhood Abandonment Issues* and would like to learn more about healing these developmental stages you may want to begin that program after completing this one – especially if your abandonment issues are severe. It is best to have a therapist, or have had some therapy, or be in an Adult/Child recovery group before starting *Thawing Childhood Abandonment Issues.*

1:3 Exploring Your Stages:

Stage One: Basic Trust vs. Mistrust *(0-2 years old)*

Positive Outcome

(I'm Ok, You're Ok)

Healthy Adult Ego-State

Negative Outcomes:

Controlling		Gullible/Naive
Externalizer		Internalizer

(I'm Ok, You're NOT Ok)   *(I'm NOT Ok, You're Ok)*
Angry/Defiant Child Energy   *Vulnerable/Needy Child Energy*

Check off as many as apply to you here-and-now:

____ I do not feel I have a right to ask others to meet my needs

____ Feeling close to others frightens me

____ The world feels like an unsafe and fearful place

____ I have a strong need to be in control in order to feel safe

____ I don't like affectionate touch or touching others (hugs, kisses)

____ I have a hard time acknowledging and responding to my own wants and needs

____ I have a difficult time giving attention to others

____ I have a strong or excessive need to be admired by others

____ Despite what others say, I doubt that I'm lovable

____ I have difficulty trusting others even if they are trustworthy

____ I lack trust in myself to take care of my needs

____ I do not trust others to care about or respond to my needs

____ I have a tendency to lose hope or feel hopeless about ever being happy or getting what I really want

____ I have a tendency to trust too early in a relationship or friendship

____ I have deep fears of intimacy because it could result in abandonment

(Write as much as you can in your journal about these answers.)

64

Stage Two: Autonomy vs. Shame & Doubt (2-3 years old)

Positive Outcome

(I'm Ok, You're Ok)

Autonomy, Boundaries & Limits

Healthy Adult Ego-State

Negative Outcomes:

Shameless Needless		Shameful Needy
Externalizer		Internalizer

(I'm Ok, You're NOT Ok)   *(I'm NOT Ok, You're Ok)*
Angry/Defiant Child Energy   *Vulnerable/Needy Child Energy*

___ I seem to say "no" automatically, as if it were a reflex

___ When I do say "no" I say it abruptly or stubbornly because I fear their rejection

___ I do not say "no" to those I am close to for fear they won't like me

___ I don't say "no" to my partner because I'm afraid he or she will leave me

___ When making plans with friends, I tend to agree with whatever they say or suggest

___ If I ask someone to do something for me and they say no, I feel shame that I asked

___ I am afraid to assert myself at work. I may get fired or my boss might say no

___ If someone I care about is angry, I feel like I've done something wrong

___ I feel embarrassed if I'm with someone who makes a scene in public. I assume others will think less of me.

___ I feel smothered if someone gets too close

___ If a friend calls and is feeling sad, I feel inadequate if I can't cheer my friend up

___ I have difficulty acknowledging when I am wrong or make a mistake

___ If I need a quiet evening at home and a friend calls in need of company, I will still agree to get together

___ If my boss asks me to work late, I say yes, even if I have other plans

___ If I ask another to do something, and say no, I feel resentful

___ I get very angry when I don't get my way

Stage Three: *Initiative vs. Guilt* *(3.5 - 7 years old)*

Positive Outcome

(I'm Ok, You're Ok)

Enterprising
&
Assertive

Healthy Adult Ego-State

Negative Outcomes:

Aggressive		Passive
Externalizer		Internalizer

(I'm Ok, You're NOT Ok)   *(I'm NOT Ok, You're Ok)*
Angry/Defiant Child Energy   *Vulnerable/Needy Child Energy*

___ I focus on things about myself that I do not like

___ If I do one thing wrong at work, I obsess about that one thing and discount any other achievements I have made during that day

___ I spend a great deal of time worrying about what others think of me

___ My internal dialog is made up of self-critical statements

___ I am very judgmental and critical of others

___ I have a hard time tolerating the imperfections of others

___ I dislike people who are too fat or too skinny

___ If I'm at a party, I feel more secure if I think I look better than most people there

___ If something goes wrong at work, I feel responsible even when it couldn't possibly be my fault

___ I believe it is conceited to say positive things about myself

___ If a friend is late, I refuse to make plans with that person again

___ If I make a mistake while participating in a new activity, I never engage in that activity again

___ When I look at my body in the mirror, I focus on what I don't like

___ I have sex with someone because it is the only way I know to feel close

___ It is easier to do a task myself than ask someone else to do it. He or she would not do it the way I want to be done anyway

___ I'm afraid to ask about something I don't understand because I'm afraid others will think I'm stupid

Stage Four: Industry vs. Inferiority (7 to Puberty)

Positive Outcome

(I'm Ok, You're Ok)

Competence & Mastery

Healthy Adult Ego-State

Negative Outcomes:

Grandiosity		Inferiority
Externalizer		Internalizer

(I'm Ok, You're NOT Ok)   *(I'm NOT Ok, You're Ok)*
Angry/Defiant Child Energy   *Vulnerable/Needy Child Energy*

___ I feel judged by or inferior to most people my age, especially those in my profession

___ I feel I have little in common with people my own age, or those in my profession

___ I feel excluded from the activities of others

___ I do not belong to organizations because I feel self-conscious

___ When I go to social gatherings, I feel out of place

___ I am more comfortable being alone than with a group of friends

___ The groups I have participated in feel closed, and I have not felt a part of the "clique"

___ I avoid certain professional positions because I would have to talk in front of others

___ I am unable to speak spontaneously in front of others. I must plan exactly what want to say before it is my turn

___ Even if I know my subject, I will not speak in public because I get too tongue-tied

___ I describe myself as a procrastinator when it comes to finishing things

___ I have sabotaged my career advancement because of my inability to meet deadlines

___ I feel clumsy participating in any sport

___ I have intense fear of making a mistake

___ I must win at any cost, or I'm terrible

___ I feel shame when I go into a nice restaurant; I feel like I don't belong

___ In team sports, I fear being chosen last

___ I refuse to participate in a sports activity in which I feel self-conscious

___ I have become a "human-doing"; achievement is the only thing that matters

Stage Five: Identity vs. Identity Diffusion (Puberty to 20)

Positive Outcome

(I'm Ok, You're Ok)

Healthy Adult Ego-State

Negative Outcomes:

More than Human		Less than Human
Extemalizer		Intemalizer

(I'm Ok, You're NOT Ok)
Angry/Defiant Child Energy

(I'm NOT Ok, You're Ok)
Vulnerable/Needy Child Energy

___ I have difficulty going to social functions alone, I feel so nervous

___ I get tongue-tied if I run into an acquaintance unexpectedly

___ When I go to party, I tend to stay pretty close to the person I came with

___ I feel too shy to talk to new people

___ I feel self-conscious in public, as if people are watching me

___ I feel uncomfortable with my body; too fat, too thin, too short, etc.

___ I am sexually inhibited

___ I like the lights off when I'm having sex

___ I feel uncomfortable when I'm around a person to whom I feel attracted

___ I need a second opinion on the decisions I make

___ If I am wearing an accessory I like and someone makes an unflattering comment, I take it off

___ If I am in a group of people, I notice the one person who does not seem to like me

___ I have a hard time trusting my own judgments, so I rely on those close to me to determine what is appropriate and essential

___When I receive news that is hard to handle, I behave in a way that later results in negative consequences

___Whenever life gets tough, I bury myself in work

___Whenever I am upset, sex is the only activity that settles me down. It doesn't matter with whom; I just know that I need that release.

___When I feel panic, I seek relief with alcohol, drugs, cigarettes, shopping, gambling, eating, etc.

___ I engage in destructive activity that has severe consequences on my finances

___If someone tries to order me around, I am unable to stand up for myself

___ I have lost jobs because when my bosses asked me to do something I did not want to do, and I reacted hastily or angrily

___ If I'm driving on the freeway and someone cuts me off, I catch up with the car and try to intimidate the driver by tailgating or yelling profanities

___ If I'm losing an argument, I storm out of the room and refuse to discuss the matter any further

___ If my boss asked me to do something that I do not want to do, I will agree but then forget or fail to complete the job

___ If the driver behind me flashes his lights indicating he wants me to move out of the fast lane, I ignore him/her and slow down even more

___ If my partner or spouse behaves in a way I do not like, I will retaliate by spending money, not coming home, or secretly going out with someone else

___ I am very concerned with what my partner or spouse wears in public

___ I get angry at my partner or supervisor when confronted with the way I behave

___ I agree with the political beliefs of those close to me

___ Even if I do not like the styles, I buy clothes that the magazines say are the most fashionable because I want to fit in and be like everyone else

___ I feel if you saw me in a crowd, you would not notice me because there's nothing about me that stands out

Stage Six: Intimacy vs. Isolation (20 -30)

Positive Outcome

(I'm Ok, You're Ok)

Intimacy, Authenticity, Responsibility

Healthy Adult Ego-State

All Negative Outcomes Reinforced & Strengthened:

All-About-Me		All-About-You
Externalizer		Internalizer

(I'm Ok, You're NOT Ok)
Angry/Defiant Child Energy   *(I'm NOT Ok, You're Ok)*
                                                 Vulnerable/Needy Child Energy

___ I rely on others to pay my rent, utilities, and food

___ I am irresponsible about paying monthly bills on time

___ I do not take care of my laundry, prepare my meals, and clean or contribute to cleaning my home

___ When someone asked me to do something even though I agree, I do not follow through

___ I am a giver in relationships; I'd like to receive, but it seems I never end up with anyone who knows how or wants to give. I often wonder if my "picker" is broken.

___ I would be considered a receiver in my relationships; I find it hard to give

___ I need to be the center of attention

___ I get very upset when things don't go my way

___When I get parking or speeding tickets, I do not pay them on time

___ If I cannot keep an appointment, instead of calling to cancel, I just do not show up

___ If I harm or damage something that does not belong to me, I remain quiet and hope the owner does not notice

___ I feel dissatisfied with where I am in my professional growth

___ I feel unmotivated to pursue the credentials I need for the career I want

___ I do not select jobs that fully reflect my professional capabilities

___ I am not successful in my relationships with coworkers

Stage Seven: Generativity vs. Stagnation (30 – 60 or 70)

Positive Outcome

(I'm Ok, You're Ok)

Giving Back to Next Generation

Healthy Adult Ego-State

Negative Outcomes of Unfinished Business:

Self-Indulgence		Self-Denial Martyr
Externalizer		Internalizer

(I'm Ok, You're NOT Ok)   *(I'm NOT Ok, You're Ok)*
Angry/Defiant Child Energy   *Vulnerable/Needy Child Energy*

In the ideal situation, it is during middle adulthood that we tend to get more involved in our community. At first it is to further our standing or career that we pursue our place in the world. Once we feel secure in our life and feel we have something to offer we gravitate toward helping others, mentoring opportunities, charity work, and generally finding some way to contribute and make a positive impact. Legacy issues drive this era of our life; we want to leave a mark and fulfill our purpose in life.

However, when we have come from the roots of dysfunction we get even more entrenched in the negative outcomes of our most formative years. *If we choose not to acknowledge and deal with these issues* from the past, they fester and grow. The phenomenon of the "mid-life crisis" is actually a recycling of earlier stages of development – buying the red sports car we always wanted or acting like a kid again is an unconscious attempt to re-do some unfinished business from our past. Addictions, obsessions, and compulsions are often the problems that keep us stuck and unable to break out of those old patterns of dysfunction and relationship styles.

Stage Eight: Ego-Integrity vs. Despair (Above 70)

Positive Outcome

(I'm Ok, You're Ok)

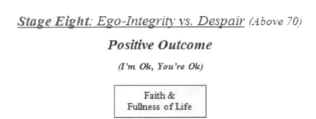

Healthy Adult Ego-State

Negative Outcomes of Unfinished Business:

(I'm Ok, You're NOT Ok)   *(I'm NOT Ok, You're Ok)*
Angry/Defiant Child Energy   *Vulnerable/Needy Child Energy*

At the end of life we have a lot of time to review. We sit on the porch and look back on our timeline here in this world. Some of us contemplate what is to come in the hereafter. A life well-lived is easier to look back on than one of regrets and missed opportunities. It is by this time that we will have reached self-actualization, or not. Will you still be living your life in reaction to the whims and moods of others? Just getting by on survival skills and self-preservation? Or will you be looking back on all that you have achieved and accomplished on the road to your recovery from abandonment, shame, and contempt?

And what is "self-actualization" anyway? Without faith, I am not sure I could answer that question. But because of what I have learned and continue to learn on this journey of life, I know that God, as I understand Him, will be with me every step of the way … and that what comes next is tremendously exciting! I know all this because He says "I will never leave nor forsake you." Now, either He meant what he said or he didn't – and NEVER is a long time. Imagine you have 97 years of wisdom, sitting in your rocking chair looking back over your life … **what do you want to see?**

Journal Exercise – If you have not already been doing so, record anything that stands out as an issue for you in your journal. Make a few notes about your thoughts and feelings concerning what you have found in each stage. Notice and explore which stages seem especially problematic to you.

Now make a list. The headings are for each stage of development where you have more than one or two items checked off. Leave room to list the checked items and anything you feel is significant from your notes and observations under each heading. This will give you a developmental inventory; i.e., issues and symptoms.

1:4 Core Issues & Developmental Processes

We human beings tend to learn, grow, and develop in stages. There are developmental stages for every important aspects of being human. Below are four of the most critical developmental processes we go through:

- **Stages of Childhood**
- **Stages of Adolescence**
- **General Life Stages**
- **Stages of a Healthy Relationship**

72

We can use these stages as a compass to mark where we are in the process of growth. We can also have some idea of what to expect, or what's "normal" for a specific stage of growth. As John Bradshaw frequently points out, each of the developmental processes listed above fit nicely into stages of a specific, predictable, and recurring higher-level developmental process – They are "stages-within-stages," if you will. These **higher-level stages** and how each of the above four processes fit into each stage are listed below:

1. **Healthy Codependence**
   - *Childhood* – Infancy, codependent with mother during infancy.
   - *Adolescence* – Individuation, codependent with peer group or a romantic involvement.
   - *General Life Stages* – Generally codependent during childhood
   - *Long-Term Relationship Stages* – Healthy codependence during courtship

2. **Healthy Counter-Dependence**
   - *Childhood* – Toddler, counter-dependent... "Terrible two's"
   - *Adolescence* – Separation, counter-dependent with family
   - *General Life Stages* – Generally counter-dependent during adolescence
   - *Long-Term Relationship Stages* – Healthy counter-dependence during Disillusionment & Conflict stage

3. **Independence**
   - *Childhood* – Pre-school, more able to play away from mother.
   - *Adolescence* – Rebellion, breaking the apron strings
   - *General Life Stages* – Young adulthood, out on their own

- *Long-Term Relationship Stages* – Independence; *"I have my life, you have your life, and we have our life"*

4. Interdependence

- *Childhood* – School-aged, getting along with peers and learning how to be part of a group
- *Adolescence* – Cooperation; begins to cooperate with the world by working together with others to reach personal goals
- *General Life Stages* – Middle Adulthood to Wisdom
- *Long-Term Relationship Stages* – Intimacy; can finish each other's sentences while maintaining a separate sense-of-self

On the following page is a chart summarizing how these developmental processes fit together. Each period of life represents the degree of separation one is able to establish. Each developmental period is also an opportunity to rework separation issues from the previous period.

Chart of Developmental Processes*

Healthy Codependence	Counter-Dependence	Independence	Interdependence
Childhood			
Infancy (0-20 months)	Toddler (2 to 4 years)	Pre-Schooler (4 to 6 years)	School-age (6 to 13 years)
Adolescence			
Individuation (13 to 14 years) With peer group	Separation (13 to 14 years) With family	Rebellion (15 to 17 years) Establishing Identity	Cooperation (18 to 26 years)
General Life Stages (Every 13 yrs)			
Childhood (0 to 13 years)	Adolescence (13 to 26 years)	Young Adulthood (26 to 39 years)	Middle/Late Adulthood (39 to Wisdom)
Long-Term Relationship			
Infatuation (24 months)	Disillusionment & Conflict	My life, Your life Our Life	Intimacy (20 years)

*As described in John Bradshaw's DVD *Post Romantic Stress Disorder* (Order at JohnBradshaw.com)

If a child is not allowed to establish enough separateness by the end of the infancy period it sets the stage for the development of *unhealthy codependency* in all of the other stages. Likewise, if a child is not allowed to establish enough separation (autonomy) by the end of the toddler stage it can lead to problems with *unhealthy counter-dependency* in all the other stages.

Given all this, it is not surprising that we "do love" according to the outcomes of these other stages.

1.4.1 Bradshaw's Four Stages of a Healthy Relationship

- **Infatuation** – This is the "Honeymoon" or courtship period. It's a time when the biological processes involved with procreation are most pronounced. Bradshaw points out that this is when the brain is being bathed in testosterone, dopamine, and other internal feel-good chemicals. Some people even report feeling dizzy or like their head is spinning during this stage.

  > There is a healthy codependency as the two merge emotionally into one ... this over-connection is intoxicating. They may want to spend all their time together ... can't stop thinking about each other, etc. In this period it may actually be "cute" to notice that your new partner has a habit of leaving the cap off the toothpaste.

  > Since the feelings are so strong there is a tendency to idealize the other person because *no one else can make me feel this way*. There is peace and harmony because your new mate *can do no wrong*. But eventually the chemical bath subsides (usually in three to six months) it paves the way for disillusionment and conflict.

- **Disillusionment & Conflict** – In this stage the "honeymoon is over" and reality sets in as our bio-chemistry returns to its normal steady-state. Now I suddenly realize that leaving the cap off the toothpaste really bugs me. It's not cute anymore and I don't have to take it!

Even the healthiest relationships go through this period of conflict early on. It's a time when neural networks are being updated and new ones created in order to adjust to living with someone. There is an instinctive jockeying for position in the newly forming status-quo. Just remember, it's a normal relationship stage and "this too will pass."

The fighting in this stage is healthy counter-dependency. It's healthy because it helps us to separate a bit from the over-connectedness of courtship. Major life changes always bring on extra stress ... even good changes. When we are under ongoing stress the "fight or flight" response can be triggered easily and often. If we are aware that this relationship stage is normal it's much easier to work through. If we are unaware, then we might wake up one morning and say things like ... *"Oh...my...god!! What have I gotten myself into?"* (Isn't it interesting how we automatically want to pray when we're in trouble?)

In this stage of the relationship, we have gathered a list of negative things about our partner that we "never noticed before." It's a good time to remember this statement: *"Whoever you are in a relationship with says as much about you as it does them."* Most relationships don't make it through this stage; those that do are usually very fortunate. If the Chemistry of Drama exists in the relationship, there is a ninety-plus percent chance it will fail in this stage (although many people can get stuck in this stage for a long, long time!).

- **Independence** – *"My life, Your Life, Our Life"* If we make it to this stage we have a good chance of staying in it for the long haul. This is where we establish healthy boundaries – a good balance of separateness and connectedness. I have my life, you have your life, and we have our life.

We have pretty much accepted most of the blemishes of our partner and love them anyway. People in a healthy relationship can do that, you know – love someone even though they don't like some things about him or her. It's called *differentiation* and it is a sign that you are very close to true intimacy.

- **Intimacy** – This is the most elusive of the relationship stages. In my opinion true intimacy is the ability to share who you really are with another person. This implies they are able to share who they really are with you. Intimacy may take up to fifteen or twenty years to develop, depending on the investment both people make in the relationship. In this stage you know each other so well that you can finish each other's sentences, but you still enjoy talking to each other anyway.

Still, longevity alone is no guarantee that a couple has achieved intimacy. There have been many people married for twenty-five or more years who never really knew one another. If you grew up in a less-than-nurturing family, chance are that you don't even know who you really are, yet (your *True Self*) – so how can you share that with another human being?

Journal Exercise Take a moment to review your relationship timeline/history. What stage or stages have you experienced in your adult relationships? Do you notice a pattern from one relationship to the other? What other thoughts come up as you explore these issues?

1.5 The Iceberg, Identification, & Intimacy

If true intimacy is indeed the ability to share who we really are with another person, then what is that "chemistry" that draws and holds us together in a dysfunctional relationship? To answer this question, let's return to an example on page 127 of *Thawing Adult/Child Syndrome*:

"…Let's look at the condition referred to as codependency; when someone has codependency their subconscious doorman (RAS) is **programmed to sort and screen for data that will support their mental filters** – *codependent values, codependent beliefs, codependent memories and experiences, codependent programs, and codependent survival skills*:

- **Values** – Please others, self-sacrifice (Be Strong), be perfect, staying busy (Work Hard)
- **Beliefs** – "I'm not good enough," "others are more important than I am," "I must always please others," "if I say "'no'" you will go away and not come back"
- **Memories & Experiences** – abandonment experiences, memories of abuse, shameful experiences, repetition compulsions,
- **Programs** – Here's how to care-take others, rescue others, control the outcomes, (Try Hard) to fix others, (Please Others and Hurry up about it!)
- **Survival Skills** – Injunctions, counter-injunctions, and Script elements, approval seeking, don't feel, don't talk, don't trust, etc.

Now let's say that this person has just ended her most recent codependent relationship. Hoping for better luck this time she begins looking for a new partner. She walks into a room full of fifty available men; forty-nine of them are healthy and only one of them is alcoholic. She is bound-and-determined to find Mr. Right this time. Who do you think she ends up with? That's right; she soon finds herself wrapped up with another alcoholic partner. She asks herself, "Why does this keep happening to me? Do I have a stamp on my forehead, or what?"

No, she doesn't have a stamp on her forehead; she has **radar** at the base of her skull, and it's called the "reticular activating system" (RAS). Her subconscious doorman is sifting through two million bits of data per second, *allowing in only that data which* *fits her codependent map of the world.* It just so happens that a person with a codependent map is extremely compatible with someone who has a map for alcoholism or other similar dysfunction. So, he is as drawn to her as she is to him – and so the sparks fly!

As I already mentioned, I have taken countless relationship histories from codependent men and women over the past twenty-seven years. I make it a point to ask, *"Was there never anyone who treated your right and was good to you?"* It never fails that *"Well, there was that one person...why don't I ever go for that type?"* I then ask how long that relationship lasted and how it ended. Invariably there is an answer very similar to, *"I don't know, we just didn't click"* or *"It just never went anywhere."* The relationships usually lasted anywhere from three weeks to three or four months.

We all know that "chemistry" must be there for two people to "click" – but what is chemistry? I think it's that *"...**radar** at the base of her skull... called the reticular activating system (RAS)..."* In the above example, all of her filters are set for codependency. It can be no other way because that's how her *"map of the world"* regarding relationships, or her ***"Love Map,"*** is set up. When she walked into the room, her doorman began sifting through two million bits of data per second – allowing in only that data which fits her codependent neural network. Consciously she had no intention of coming anywhere close to another alcoholic. Consciously she really was looking for Mr. Right and the happily-ever-after scenario. It just so happens that a person with a codependent love-map is extremely compatible with someone who has a map for alcoholism or other similar dysfunction. So, as he leaks two million bits of data out of his pores like pheromones, his mental filters draw him to her just as she is drawn to him – i.e., ***they have "chemistry."*** Her love-map subconsciously synchronizes with his and they dance the only dance they both know.

The model below shows how this dysfunctional connection is made. It is through this connection that we eventually begin acting-out cycles of abandonment, shame, and contempt. Remember that even in healthy relationships there is a period of coming together ("chemistry") in to form a codependent bond called **infatuation**. Testosterone and dopamine, along with other feel-good opiate neurotransmitters flood the system in this phase. When we feel this good we want it to last. So we work hard to "sell ourselves" to the other person during the courtship phase. We are connecting from behind the mask of our invented self; our public image – not yet sharing who we really are.

Cycles of Abandonment, Shame, & Contempt

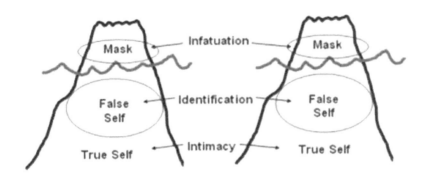

Eventually however, someone has to take a chance, remove the mask, and share something risky. There is considerable fear that accompanies such self-disclosures – a fear that the other person will run screaming down the street and never come back! But that doesn't happen. In fact, the other person is compelled to share something equally risky. Before you know it the whole night has passed and the sun is coming up – and they were so busy talking that they didn't even have sex!

It is a very powerful feeling to take such a risk only to discover that the other person didn't leave. In fact, they actually understood and accepted "all my worst stuff" because they have been there and done that too! It is such a powerful feeling that we mistake it for true intimacy. But remember, true **intimacy** is sharing *who we really are* with each other. In this case, two people shared their False Selves with each other; they shared their pain, and fears, and shame, and *who they thought they were* with each other. This may be intense, but it is NOT true intimacy, it's called **identification**, and it is very powerful. It cannot last because as long as the abandonment, shame, and contempt remains, the wounds will eventually get "triggered" and the cycles begin. Take a moment to consider the Chemistry of Drama and how it magnifies everything in the disillusionment stage. It is no wonder most relationships don't make it past that point!

1.6 Five Drivers & the Figure Eight

In *Thawing Adult/Child Syndrome* we learned about what are known in TA as **"The Five Drivers."** These counter-injunctions get this name because they "drive" us relentlessly, just beneath the surface of our awareness. These inner mandates are at the core of why we do those things we don't consciously authorize that leave us asking ourselves *"Why do I do that?"* or *"When will this ever go away?"* Most, if not all, counter-injunctions can fit into one or a combination of the first five listed below; six and seven are examples of combinations of the first five:

1. **Be Strong**
2. **Be Perfect**
3. **Try Hard**
4. **Please Others**
5. **Hurry Up**
6. **Work Hard** (a combination of Try Hard + Please Others)
7. **Don't ask for what you need** (a combination of Be Strong + Try Hard)

These **Five Drivers** "drive" survival role behaviors by providing internal pressure in the form of anxiety and stress when they are disobeyed or resisted. This pressure may be reminiscent of the feeling of "being in trouble" with authority figures from childhood. Conversely, these Drivers provide a **"Safety Net of Ok-ness"** *as long as we obey them*. As long as we *stay in the Driver behavior* we can "feel somewhat Ok" because the Drivers help us ward off the shame-based messages of the Critical Parent.

As long as people can keep the mask of their <u>Invented-Self</u> on by fulfilling these driver behaviors they can **feel OK**. But as soon as they slip up and violate one of these inner mandates, even if only once, they drop through the **safety net of "Ok-ness"** provided by the Driver behaviors into the territory of the <u>False-Self</u> where they experience feeling bad or **"NOT Ok"** anymore – often referred to as being "triggered" and known in TA as the "rubber-band effect" because it's like being "rubber-banded" back into a childhood experience.

The **Figure-Eight** model [Diagram 1] below is a visual representation of this triggering process. The first thing we notice about the model is that both parties have somewhat equal amounts of abandonment, shame, and contempt. This is due to the issues of chemistry and that radar at the base of the skull known as the RAS described in Section 1:4 above. We attract partners who fit our love-map and do not experience that chemistry without a successful subconscious audition. When the sparks fly and we fall for each other, the dance begins.

Eventually, when one party gets triggered, different kinds of sparks begin to fly! And this is an important thing to notice – "sparks" of course, represent **intensity**. Sparks of the first kind are positive intensity and sparks of the second kind are negative intensity. And those of us who come from a dysfunctional background *mistake intensity for intimacy – and negative intensity is better than no intensity!* We will come back to this core issue later on.

In Diagram 1 below, the "A" represents the activating event or "trigger" that sets a cycle of abandonment, shame, and contempt into motion. Something happens between the two parties. It could be anything at all. It could be a simple mannerism such as the raising of an eyebrow, or a tone of voice, or anything else that triggers the abandonment, shame, and contempt.

I know of a couple who was sitting on a sofa watching a movie. She got thirsty and got up to get a drink from the other room and he was surprised to notice that he suddenly felt abandoned. The simple act of her getting up and walking out of the room triggered his abandonment issues.

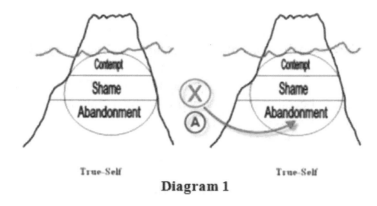

Diagram 1

In Neuro Linguistic Programming (NLP) they refer to the trigger as an anchor. An example of an auditory anchor is when you hear an old song that sends you back into the memories of bygone days. An example of a visual anchor is the above example of seeing someone walk away and feeling abandoned. A key point here is that no one "makes me feel" abandonment, shame, and contempt – *I already have feelings of abandonment, shame, and contempt.* There is no way to sterilize my environment from "triggering" anchors. In fact, if I am in a dysfunctional relationship I am in a trigger-rich environment!

In Diagram 2 below, "B" represents the beliefs and self-talk that automatically begin when triggered. This is the meaning I make of the thing that just happened between us. And, of course, the judge of "what just happened" is our Critical Parent ego-state.

And the Critical Parent uses shame-based perception and psychological positions to interpret what just happened. If the shame-laden self-talk is focused on blaming the other person, then Angry/Defiant Child energy takes over and contempt is directed toward that other person. Conversely, if the shaming self-talk is directed inward toward the self, then Vulnerable/Needy Child energy is stirred up.

The "C" in the diagram represents the behavioral outcome of the beliefs and self-talk. If I am primarily an Internalizer my Vulnerable/Needy ego-state will accept the shame and affirm the Critical Parent messages, which has the effect of increasing the pain – the internalization becomes the next "A" or activating event that keeps the cycle going. This can be referred to as "acting-in" because it affects only the Internalizer.

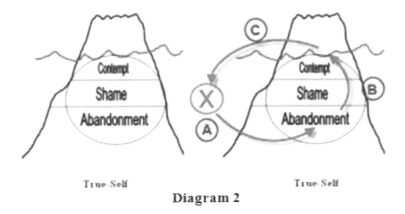

Diagram 2

Sooner or later the build-up from internalization will reach a threshold. Usually the person will then "act-out" or "blow-up" at the partner as depicted in Diagram 3. The behavioral outcome "C" of this blow-up will become the "A" for the person being on the receiving end of the blow-up. This frequently comes as a surprise and catches the person off guard because the person may not have even realized the partner was holding all of this in.

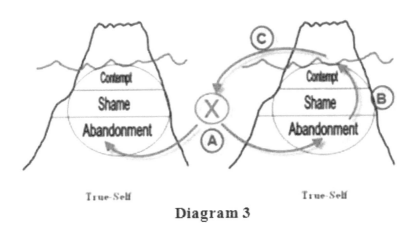

Diagram 3

The final move below completes the Figure-Eight and a full blown battle is at hand. The triggered partner internalizes until he or she can't hold the Critical Parent and/or Angry Child energy back anymore or simply returns the favor by immediately blowing up at the offending party, externalizing abandonment, shame, and contempt as shown in Diagram 4 below.

This creates the new "A" for the offending party and the battle is on. Acting out each cycle goes on until a ceasefire occurs. This usually concludes with a threat of abandonment by one partner or the other. The length and severity of an episode can heap even more abandonment, shame, and contempt on each of the participants until, ultimately, the relationship falls apart.

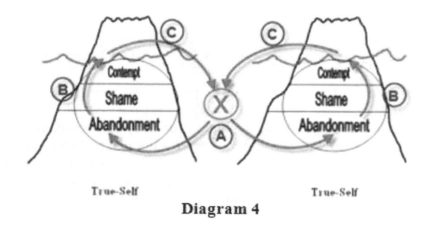

True-Self   True-Self

Diagram 4

In summary, while there may have been an initial trigger for the cycle, both parties keep it going as they *fall through the "Safety net of Ok-ness" into the "Not Ok" territory of the False Self* (see *Thawing Adult/Child Syndrome*, p. 76).

Falling Through the Safety Net

The seemingly universal word for falling through the safety net provided by the drivers is "triggered." Most people automatically know what that term means. In TA the concept is seen as "shifting ego-states." We move from the emotional state of feeling "Ok" into the "NOT Ok" feelings that produce the Chemistry of Drama!

There are four ways to act upon the Not-Ok feelings. Three of them produced the chemistry of drama and the fourth one is the only one that qualifies as suitable for true intimacy in a mature relationship (except in a few rare instances such as survival situations). Let's first understand the symbols below:

(I) = *I'm,*
(U) = *You're,*
(-) = *NOT Ok,*
(+) = *Ok*

Four Styles of Coping with Triggers:

1   **Blaming (I+, U-):** *Externalizing the Not-Ok feelings* of abandonment, shame and contempt by entertaining Critical Parent (CP) self-talk about how the other(s) are "making you feel" that way. This stirs up the *Angry/Defiant Child energy* which mixes with the CP messages and is directed outward at the other(s).

2   **Surrendering (I-, U+):** *Internalizing the NOT-Okfeelings* of abandonment, shame, and contempt by giving into the inwardly directed Critical Parent self-talk about how *"...You are never going to get what you want/need, or how you are unlovable, unworthy,"* *etc.* This, of course, is experienced as Internalization of the *Vulnerable/Needy Child energy.*

3   **Panicking (I-, U-):** *Simultaneously Internalizing and Externalizing the NOT-Ok feelings* of hopelessness, helplessness, and worthlessness of the futility position while experiencing Critical Parent messages about the "Not Ok-ness" of self, others, and the world at large (causing a sense of

desperation and/or urgency from *rapid cycling between Vulnerable Child energy and Angry/Defiant child energy*).

4   **Healthy Coping: (I+, U+):** *Notice the potential trigger and choose to stay in the Adult Ego-State* bringing the full power of your adult problem-solving and decision-making resources to bear on the situation without making it about the Ok-ness of self or other. Having your feelings but not letting them "drive your bus." Learning to detach enough to remain objective and rational even when the situation may be unacceptable (i.e., Not Ok).

It is common to find that you have experienced all of these reactions and psychological positions at different times. Many times, at some level of awareness, we are experiencing two or more positions simultaneously. Take, for instance, the core issue of Psychological Sweatshirts.

Journal Exercise: Take a moment to review your relationship timeline/history again. Which do you relate to your own style or patterns of coping when triggered: **Blaming, Surrendering, Panicking, Healthy Coping.**

How might you relate the Five Drivers and the Figure Eight to yourself and in your adult relationships? How do these fit your memories of how your parents related to each other? How do they fit with how one or both parents related to you and your siblings? Do you notice a pattern from one relationship to another? What thoughts come up as you explore these issues?

1.7 Psychological Sweatshirts

The founder of Transactional Analysis, Eric Berne, MD, often talked about his analogy of **Psychological Sweatshirts**. He used this analogy to explain how a person can hold two existential or psychological positions simultaneously. One position is usually explicit (conscious) and the other implicit (subconscious). The analogy is to *imagine a person wearing a sweatshirt that has an explicit message on the front and an implicit message on the back.* Each message represents its own existential position – usually conflicting messages. Here are some examples of TA Sweatshirts:

Front: "Someone please love me!" **Back**: "Not you stupid!'"
Front: "Keep your distance!" **Back**: "A little closer please'"
Front: "I'm special, admire me!" **Back**: "Kick Me"
Front: "Whatever you say is fine – really!" **Back**: "Now I've Got You, You SOB!
Front: "Please tell me what to do" **Back**: "So I can tell you why that can't work."
Front: "I hate you!" **Back**: "Please don't leave me!"

Psychological Sweatshirts are often *the result of disowning one ego-state*, usually the *Angry/Defiant Child* or the *Vulnerable Child ego-state*, which has the effect of magnifying the ego state that operates at a conscious level. Sweatshirts are also good representations for the nature of psychological mind games one subconsciously initiates and participates in. Many times the only way you can tell you've been part of a subconscious mind game is the surprise bad feeling you get after it's over. The game can start as an innocent question but ends with a bad feeling in your stomach – and you haven't a clue about what just happened.

The "surprise bad feeling," aka Primary Scripty Feeling, is known in TA as the "payoff" for playing mind games – the Scripty Feeling Payoff is frequently a somewhat irritating, yet weirdly satisfying, feeling that confirms your psychological position. You can learn more about Scripty Feelings and confirmation of psychological positions by review of the work you did in *Thawing Adult/Child Syndrome* (Section 2.3.2, p. 80).

Journal Exercise: Take a moment to review your relationship history again. What occurs to you regarding **Sweatshirts and disowning ego-states** in your adult relationships? Do you notice a pattern from one relationship to the other? What other thoughts come up as you explore these issues

How might you relate Sweatshirts and disowning ego-states to yourself and in your adult relationships? How do these fit your memories of how your parents related to each other? How do they fit with how one or both parents related to you and your siblings? Do you notice a pattern from one relationship to another? What thoughts come up as you explore these issues?

1.8 Polarization – Disowned & Borrowed Parts

There is another core issue that springs from disowned ego-states that has a major role in the type of relationship we find ourselves in. When I disown a part of my personality, I am attracted to that quality in a partner. It is as if I borrow what I have "lost" from the other person, and the other person is likely to have disowned the opposite part of themselves which they "borrow" from me – this is referred to as **Polarization** and it is why "opposites attract." Below are some examples of disowned and borrowed parts.

- *Overly Responsible Person and Fun-Loving Addict* – Overly responsible partners subconsciously and vicariously experience their disowned "fun-and-spontaneity" part through their partners while addicts subconsciously and vicariously experience their disowned "responsible" parts through their partners.
- *Excessively Emotional Person and Emotionally Distant Mate* – Excessively emotional partners subconsciously and vicariously experience their disowned "emotional-regulation" part through their partners while emotionally distant partners subconsciously and vicariously experience their disowned "emotional-expression" parts through their partners.
- *Flammable Person and Calm/Cool/Collected Mate* – Partners with a flammable temper subconsciously and vicariously experience their disowned "composure-maintaining" parts through their partners while Calm/Cool/Collected partners subconsciously and

vicariously experience their disowned "anger-releasing" parts through their partners.

- *Excessively Nice (Edith Bunker) and Hostile Mate (Archie)* – Overly-nice partners subconsciously and vicariously experience their disowned "hostility" through their partners; hostile partners subconsciously and vicariously experience their disowned "soft-and-compassionate" parts through their partners.
- *Passive Person and Aggressive Mate* – Passive partners subconsciously and vicariously experience their disowned "empowering" parts through their partners while aggressive partners subconsciously and vicariously experience their disowned "humility-and-restraint" parts through their partners.
- *Givers and Takers* – Giving partners subconsciously and vicariously experience their disowned ""love-receiving" parts through their partners while taking partners subconsciously and vicariously experience their disowned "love-giving" parts through their partners.

Journal Exercise: Look back over your relationship history. Do you see any issues regarding such an imbalance or **polarization** in any of your relationships? Is there a pattern?

How might you relate the concept of Polarization to yourself and in your adult relationships? How do these fit your memories of how your parents related to each other? How do they fit with how one or both parents related to you and your siblings? Do you notice a pattern from one relationship to another? What thoughts come up as you explore these issues?

1.9 Emotional Themes & Mini Script Processes

According to TA theorists such as founder Eric Berne, Taibi Kahler and other TA authors such as Stewart and Joines, (1987) there are only six main patterns of Script Process. You did some work on these emotional themes that play out over and over in your life in *Thawing Adult/Child Syndrome* (Section 2.5, p. 98).

These core issues are listed below.

Until: **Motto**: *"I can't have fun **until** I've finished my work"*

> **Principle**: Something good can't happen until something less good has been finished.
> *Examples*:
> - Once the kids grow up and leave I'll be able to take time for me
> - Life begins after forty
> - After I make a fortune, then I can retire, travel and enjoy life
> - After I fully understand myself then I can change

After: **Motto:** *"I'll have fun today **but** I'll pay for it tomorrow"*

> **Principle**: The sentence begins with a "high" then there is a fulcrum (usually the word "but") followed by a "low."
> *Examples:*
> - Have your fun now, after you get married the honeymoon is over"
> - Wow, this is a great party! But I am going to be sick as a dog tomorrow!"

Almost: **Motto:** *"I almost made it this time!"*

> **Principle**: Great at starting something, gets almost done, but doesn't finish
> *Examples:*
> - **Type One**: Like pushing a big rock up a hillside, gets almost to the top, loses grip and it rolls back down again
> - **Type Two**: Like pushing a big rock up a hillside, notices a bigger rock and taller hillside and jumps to that one, letting the other roll back down again

Always: **Motto:** *"Bad things always happen to me"*

Principle: "If something can go wrong it will"

Examples:

- "Why do I always miss out on the fun?"
- Why does this always have to happen to me?"

Never: **Motto:** *"I will never get what I want or need"*

Principle: "The more I want it, the more I can't have it."

Examples:

- I'll never get that promotion
- I'll never find anyone to love me
- There's never enough (Love, Money, Time, etc.)

Open-Ended: *Variation on the "Until" and "After" themes* in that there is a Tipping point after which things change. But after that cutoff there is a big empty void.

Examples:

- **"After"** finishing a project the person flounders, not knowing what to do next… **"Until"** another project comes along.

Script Drivers & Mini-Script Processes

Script Drivers also seem to be paired with the script processes. When you discover one it is highly likely that you have the counter-part as well.

Drivers	**(Mini Scripts)**
Be Perfect!	(Until)
Please Others!	(After)
Be Strong!	(Never)
Try Hard!	(Always)
Please Others! + Try Hard!	(Almost Type 1)
Be Perfect! + Try Hard!	(Almost Type 2)
Be Perfect! + Please Others!	(Open-ended)
Hurry-Up!	(Open-ended, Until)

Journal Exercise: Review the work you did on "Drivers and Your Mini-Script Processes" in *Thawing Adult/Child Syndrome* (Section 2.5, p. 98). How do you see or feel these emotional themes playing out in your adult relationships? Do you see of feel any patterns? Are your partners compatible with your Drivers and Mini-Scripts?

How might you relate these Driver/Mini-Script combinations to yourself and in your adult relationships? How do these fit your memories of how your parents related to each other? How do they fit with how one or both parents related to you and your siblings? Do you notice a pattern from one relationship to another? What thoughts come up as you explore these issues?

1.10   Summary of Core Relationship Issues

Let's stop for a moment to consolidate what you have learned about the core issues that block you from achieving the kind of relationship you want. As you fill in the blanks below keep in mind this is YOUR inventory of core issues, not your partner's inventory. They must do their own work and you can only be responsible for cleaning up your side of the street.

Here is something to consider as you move forward with recovery. If your partner chooses not to engage in this work then it is likely that one of two things will result: either your partner will join you later as the benefits as reflected through you; or your partner will leave to go find another partner who knows how to dance the dance you are no longer dancing. Having said that, if you still want to proceed, then fill in the blanks below with your best answers (write these out in your Journal).

I. Do you identify yourself as an Internalizer or Externalizer? Why or Why Not? (p. 55)

II. Do you tend to distance or pursue in relationships? Do you tend to join with a pursuer or distancer? Give examples. (p. 56)

III. Can you relate to and identify a familiar cycle that produces the Chemistry of Drama? Describe your pattern as best you can. (pp. 57-59)

IV. Do you identify primarily as a co-dependent or counter-dependent? Which if either? Why or why not? (p. 61)

V. Which psychological position(s) are you most familiar with? Do you experience other positions depending on which ego-state is active? (pp. 62-64)

VI. Developmental Stages: List and explore any core issues you have found in the following stages: (pp. 68-75)

    a. Stage One, Trust vs. Mistrust
    b. Stage Two, Autonomy vs. Shame and Doubt
    c. Stage Three, Initiative vs. Guilt
    d. Stage Four, Industry vs. Inferiority
    e. Stage Five, Identity, vs. Identity Confusion
    f. Stage Six, Intimacy vs. Isolation
    g. Stage Seven, Generativity vs. Stagnation
    h. Stage Eight, Ego-Integrity vs. Despair

VII. What have you uncovered about your history with the four stages of a healthy relationship? Have you ever made it past stage two? If not, what significant patterns stand out about your experiences? (p. 82)

VIII. What stands out about what you learned about yourself regarding Infatuation, Identification, and Intimacy? (pp. 83-85)

IX. What are your most powerful Drivers? What happens when you disobey one of those drivers and "fall through" their safety net, i.e., when you get triggered? What Figure Eight Cycles (Activating Events, Beliefs, and Consequences) do you see in your history of relationships? (pp. 86-91)

X. What is your Primary Coping style or reaction when you get triggered? Are there secondary reactions or styles that frequently occur? (pp. 92)

XI. Have you identified a Psychological Sweatshirt that might fit you? How about one that would fit the partners you have had in your life? (pp. 93-94)

XII. What stands out about Polarization, i.e., disowned and borrowed parts, regarding your history of relationships? (p. 95)

XIII. What Emotional Themes and Mini-Script Processes are most familiar to you? (pp. 96-99)

Section 2: Self-Preservation & Passing Time

There is an old saying, *"First you are born...then you die."* It fails to mention anything about how to spend all that time between those events – because that is entirely up to us! If we come from a less-than-nurturing family, there are really only two overall choices: 1) We can spend our time in **Survival Mode** by allowing our wounded inner children to "drive our bus," or 2) We can spend our time in **Growth Mode** by reaching out for help and beginning the journey of recovery.

Survival Mode is for those times when we "get triggered" and all of our core issues come out. It is also referred to as the instinct for **Self-Preservation** (i.e., "fight or flight syndrome").

Growth Mode is for those times in life when we are pursuing our dreams, challenging ourselves, becoming all we were meant to be – also known as the instinct for **Self-Actualization.**

2.1 Structuring Time

In Self-Preservation we *operate from our False Self*; i.e., act-out the scripted behaviors (also outlined in *Thawing Adult/Child syndrome and other Codependent Patterns*) that were programmed into us from childhood to help us survive the ordeal. In Self-Actualization we *operate from our True Self* – i.e., access and apply the full power of our autonomous, problem-solving, and decision-making Adult ego-state to the here-and-now circumstances and relationships as they occur in our lives.

The scripted behaviors of our False Self are also referred to as *survival skills* because they were created by the Little Professor part of our personality in order to adapt to and survive the dysfunction in our environment. In other words, they were creative solutions designed by our instinct to survive. We can refer to this as *Self-Preservation* or survival mode. The choices we make from a clear and healthy Adult ego-state are geared toward growth. These growth-oriented choices spring from our instinct to self-actualize and become all that we can be – our True Self.

Maslow also pointed out that one cannot devote energy to growth if the need to survive is threatened; e.g., a third grader cannot concentrate on learning her math lesson if she has not had breakfast or lunch that day. So, Self-Preservation is given priority by the subconscious mind while Self-Actualization must wait until survival has been assured. *This makes it critical to develop a "safe-container" in which to grow a healthy relationship.* One cannot devote any energy to creating such in an environment where abandonment, shame, and contempt cycles persist.

The purpose of this section is to explore how and why we are likely to structure our time in ways that keep us *stuck in survival mode* if we came from a moderate to severely dysfunctional family system, especially in terms of our relationships. We will also examine what true intimacy in relationships looks like and how to achieve it.

2.1.1 The Three Hungers of the Inner Child

First let's look at the roots of our time structuring choices – Childhood. There are three things that a child does not tolerate well – *a lack of structure, a lack of stimulation, and a lack of nurturing.* Kids **need** a daily schedule of proper diet, sleep, exercise and routines (Structure). They **need** fun, adventure, and excitement (Stimulation). And they **need** time, attention, affection, and direction (Nurturing). A lack in any one of these needs causes a cranky kid and, if they repeatedly go unmet, more abandonment, shame, and contempt that follows us into adulthood.

The Child ego-state is the location of what we want, what we need, and how we feel – it is therefore necessary for us to be in touch with our Child ego-state in order to have *self-awareness*. Without self-awareness we cannot satisfy our wants and needs because we don't know what they are. Satiation of emotional needs can be compared to hunger; if we go without food long enough we will eat a piece of crusty bread if that's all that's available in order to satisfy the powerful hunger driven by self-preservation. In Transactional Analysis (TA), there are three primary "hungers" that drive our behavior:

- **Structure Hunger** – The need to structure our time in a way that helps us fulfill the following two hungers.
- **Stimulus Hunger** – Strokes, intensity, excitement, etc.
- **Position Hunger** – Confirmation of our Psychological Position (Ok...not Ok)

Notice how the first two hungers match the first two things that kids need (described above) and the third one – *Position Hunger* – is a direct result of the nurturing we get, or don't get. This is because the Child ego-state is child-created. It is created in our childhood and its "default settings" are the result of the parenting we received – how well did our parents provide structure, stimulation, and nurturing?

2.1.2 Structure Hunger

In childhood our parents lay out our clothes, tell us when to get up, when to go to bed, what to eat, what activities we will participate in (church, schools, community, etc.) and we are pretty much ok with that because we need direction as much as we do structure. In adulthood we lay out our own clothes, decide when to go to bed, when to get up, what activities we participate in etc. We are in charge of structuring our lives as fully functioning adult human-beings.

As teenagers, in between childhood and adulthood, we want to take over our own structure and our parents want to retain the job; and that's when things can get more than a little dicey. Adolescence is a long period of transition in the area of structuring our lives and how we spend our time. One way or another we end up on our own. How things went during childhood and adolescence influences how we handle structure and self-care as adults.

The primary evidence of appropriate structure is having healthy boundaries. Conversely, the inability to set and reinforce healthy boundaries is evidence of inadequate structure during developmental periods. Inadequate boundaries are weak, absent, or too rigid and more like walls than boundaries.

Weak or absent boundaries come from the disowning or discounting of the Angry/Defiant Child ego-state – the energy from the Angry/Defiant Child functions to help us say "no" and empowers us to protect ourselves while maintaining a separate sense of self. Without it, we have tremendous difficulty setting boundaries. When we discount one ego-state, the opposite ego-state gets magnified, leaving one to feel even more powerless and vulnerable.

Rigid boundaries or "walls" imprison and isolate us. If we think of boundaries as a fence around our property line, then rigid boundaries would be like the twelve-foot privacy fence. It definitely keeps people out because they cannot even see through it. But it also becomes like a prison wall because the builder is also unable to see through it, and there is no gate to in a rigid boundary – no one gets through it.

If you think of your life as a playground, a healthy boundary would be like a chain link fence around it with one gate or entrance. You can see out and others can see in, but they can only enter through the gate. On the gate is a list of rules to follow in order to come into your playground. If the visitor cannot respect the rules and the equipment on the playground, then they are invited to go elsewhere.

Healthy boundaries are firm, effective, and under the control of the person who is in charge of setting them – that would be you, as in your Adult ego-state. The Adult ego state needs to take over "driving the bus" of our lives because the Adult ego-state is the best decision-maker and problem-solver. The Adult ego-state makes the decisions and solves the problems by consulting the other ego-states and borrowing their energies to implement the action plans.

The Parent ego-state provides information to the Adult ego-state about what the Child ego-states need in the way of nurturing and protection. The Adult ego-state checks in with the Child ego-states to learn what their wants and needs are in the situation at hand. Then, upon gathering all the necessary information and considering all the available options, the Adult ego-state makes a decision and then carries it out.

But if we have Adult/Child Syndrome, we are prone to "living life in reaction"; i.e., being triggered into the Vulnerable/Needy Child or the Angry/Defiant Child ego-states. At those times we can feel unable to access our Adult resources. Living life in reaction to our triggers is so familiar it can feel normal. Learning to operate from the Adult ego-state can seem so foreign and unfamiliar. We may even be tempted to go back to the old programming.

With practice, discipline, a healthy support circle such as a community support group (i.e., a new functional family), prayer and meditation, and lots of work, we can and do heal these parts of ourselves.

Journal Exercise: Review your current and past relationships. How much structure did you have growing up in your family? Was it to loose or too rigid? Did you have to provide your own structure?

Do you currently feel able to set boundaries in your life? Are you afraid to say "no?" Are your boundaries too rigid; do you feel trapped, isolated and unable to really connect with others or let them in? Other thoughts and observations as you read about Structure Hunger?

How well do you take care of yourself? Do you eat right, exercise, and get enough sleep? Do you take care of your medical and dental needs? Do you have balance in your life? Or do you drive yourself too hard and abuse or neglect your needs? Do you take any "me time" to play and rest?"

2.1.3 Stimulus Hunger

Our Child ego-states require stimulation in the form of intensity, excitement, and adventure. If we don't get it, we may find ourselves acting-out in unhealthy ways that are very stimulating and intense, such as addictions to alcohol, drugs, sex, gambling, video games, food, spending, debting, adrenaline, drama, etc. When these things become issues in our life it is like *we periodically become like kids in a candy store without parental supervision!*

When we explore the mind games below we will see how the need for stimulation plays a major role in the abandonment, shame, and contempt cycles we find ourselves participating in with the people who we love the most. All is NOT fair in love and war! As we will see later, love and war should have nothing at all to do with one another.

Strokes & Stroking

Giving and receiving love, support, recognition, and validation is referred to in TA language as "stroking." The term was chosen by Eric Berne because physical stroking was found to be necessary for the health, growth, and even the survival of infants. As we grow older we still have a need for physical touch but we also find other ways to give and receive verbal and non-verbal strokes, such as praise, validation, smiles, etc.

But stroking can also be negative – because negative stimulation is better than no stimulation at all and in dysfunctional families sometimes negative strokes may be the only stimulation available. Hero children get the positive strokes for their flashy or responsible behavior, rebels get the negative strokes for their misbehavior, lost children get strokes through fantasy and imagination, and mascots get strokes through the verbal and non-verbal reactions of others to their silly or cute behavior.

Some examples of negative verbal strokes are the things one says when triggered into a Critical Parent or Angry/Defiant Child reaction – *"I hate you!" "You're stupid!"* Examples of typical non-verbal strokes are a rolling of the eyes or frowning. Strokes and stroking then are about stimulation and recognition.

The availability of positive and negative strokes in one's environment is referred to in TA as the *stroke economy*. A person with a scarcity of positive strokes is likely to become depressed. A person with an abundance of positive stokes is usually pretty happy. As you can probably imagine, the stroke economy in one's family can be toxic and set up negative/positive stroke cycles that result in the *Chemistry of Drama*. For example, wounded, externalizing parents may get triggered and direct angry outbursts toward their children. They may immediately follow up that outburst with an apology and a trip to the park or ice cream store to "make up" for it.

Developing a support network of people who will provide genuine positive strokes is a requisite to healing from Adult/Child

Syndrome. Learning to accept positive strokes from others is the next challenge, especially when one's self-talk is primarily critical and negative.

2.1.4 Position Hunger

We also stroke ourselves with the inner dialog we choose to entertain. Turning Critical Parent messages of shame and contempt inward is a way of giving ourselves the negative strokes we grew accustomed to in childhood. When we externalize our Critical Parent messages we give negative strokes to others. These internalized and externalized messages of shame and contempt are rooted in the childhood dysfunction of growing up with unmet emotional dependency needs for time attention, affection and direction – all of which would be considered positive strokes.

These Critical Parent strokes are the source of the Psychological Positions held by our adapted Child ego-states (i.e., Vulnerable Child, Angry/Defiant Child, and Critical Parent). As we have seen, these are the parts of our personality that hold Positions about the "Ok-ness" of self, others, and the world in general. When one of these Psychological Positions is confirmed yet again, we experience an emotional charge (stimulation). For example, responding to a mistake by someone you counted on with a self-statement such as, *"Ah ha! I knew it, you just can't trust anyone!"* (I'm Ok, People are NOT Ok!)

So, *Position Hunger* is that subconscious need to confirm these Psychological Positions and the "confirmations" come with an emotional charge that also meets our need for strokes. It is necessary to become willing to let go of, revise, or otherwise re-decide these NOT Ok Positions so that we get reinforcement for experiencing what we Do want instead of what we Don't want. This means bringing our Adult ego-state into the process so we can be objective in challenging these limiting beliefs.

In recovery from Adult/Child Syndrome we must also create realistic affirmations and permissions to develop healthy self-talk. We practice those affirmations and permissions repeatedly in order to develop the ability to override the injunctions and counter-injunctions that produce the negative stroke economy, replacing it with a positive one.

It is also critical to find ways to add excitement, adventure and intensity to our lives in healthy ways.

Journal Exercise: What kinds of strokes were you accustomed to receiving in your childhood? Which kinds of strokes are you accustomed to receiving in your adult life? What kinds of strokes do you give? Do you tend to direct your Critical Parent messages outward or inward when triggered?

Can you identify negative/positive stroke cycles in your family that lead to the development of the Chemistry of Drama in your subsequent relationships?

What are some limiting beliefs and psychological positions you hold about yourself, others and/or life in general? Are you willing to challenge those beliefs? How about the positions you hold about yourself or others that have a negative impact on your important relationships?

2.2 Six Methods of Structuring Time:

All of us, no matter how functional or dysfunctional our family was, try to avoid the pain of boredom by seeking something to do with our time. We structure time in six possible ways:

- **Withdrawal**
- **Rituals**
- **Pastimes**
- **Activities**
- **Mind Games**
- **True Intimacy**

2.2.1 Withdrawal

Withdrawing is sometimes a rational adult decision. We all need a little "Me Time" to be alone. We need time to think our own thoughts and take stock of ourselves. We need to rest, relax, and restore energy. Then we need to once again make healthy contact with another person.

At other times withdrawal becomes a dysfunctional coping style, a way to avoid contact with others. For example, Lost Children, frequently the middle children in a less-than-nurturing family dynamic, use this coping style to escape the chaos and retreat into "a world of their own." This style of coping then follows them into adulthood causing problems in their relationships.

People can withdraw from others by removing themselves in the following ways:

- **Physically** – leaving or retreating to another room
- **Psychologically** – withdrawing into fantasy, television, computers, addictions, etc.
- **Emotionally** – staying in their rational, Adult ego-state to the exclusion of any feelings from the child-created ego-states

Even withdrawal into one's fantasies is often legitimate. A good fantasy may be a better use of time than listening to a bad lecture. Withdrawal helps us take that time for "me."

Withdrawing is sometimes based on copying parents or imitating parental behavior. For example, a man threatened by conflict with his wife may withdraw as his father did when his mother got mad. He may leave the house, retire to the shop, or go to his study. Or, instead of physically leaving, he may go to sleep or simply "tune out" his wife, not even hearing what she says.

When a person withdraws psychologically, it's often into a fantasy world. These fantasies may be of uncensored pleasure or violence, creative imaginings, or of learned fears and catastrophic expectations. Extreme withdrawal can lead to isolation causing the person to have a scarcity of opportunities for healthy stroking in his or her environment which contributes to depression.

Journal Exercise: How does the concept of withdrawal as a means of structuring time strike you? Do you use withdrawal in healthy ways? Unhealthy ways? Did either of your parents use withdrawal to avoid conflict and intimacy? Do you or your partner use withdrawal as a means of avoid conflict or intimacy?

2.2.2 Rituals

Ritual interactions are simple complementary transactions between two or more people, such as greetings or goodbyes. Someone who says, "Good morning, how are you?" is not necessarily asking about other person's health and feelings. Usually the expected response is something like, "Fine, how are you?" In TA this is referred to as **a two-stroke ritual. A common six-stroke ritual may look like this:**

A: Hi
B: Hi

A: How are you?
B: Fine, and you?

A: Fine. Well, see you later.
B: Yeah, see you around.

A ritual gives people a way of coming together. They save time in figuring out who should go first, or be served first, and so forth. Some cultures, church groups, political parties, secret orders, and social clubs structure their time with highly ritualistic patterns of behavior. Other groups are less structured, using their time in other ways. For many people, rituals have become a way of life. For example, after the ceremony is long past, the marriage may only be a series of ritualistic transactions consisting mainly of role-playing, devoid of any real meaning or intimacy, yet just enough strokes to keep the marriage alive.

2.2.3 Pastimes

Pastimes are transactions people use to "pass time" with one another when they don't know each other very well. Pastimes are any safe subjects, such as the weather, the stock market, the local football team, how bad kids are today – anything that keeps things superficial.

Pastimes and rituals are "staying at arm's length" behaviors that people use to spend time together politely without getting involved at a deeper level. They provide the opportunity to get to know each other well enough to decide on further involvement in games, activities, or intimacy.

2.2.4 Activities

Activities are ways of structuring time that deal with external reality and are commonly thought of as work, getting something done, and/or staying busy. Activities are time killers people choose because they want to, need to, or have to do them. Activities can be carried out alone or with others, some examples are:

- Serving on a committee
- Playing in a band
- working on a long-term project
- Getting a master's degree
- Building a house
- Writing a book
- Engaging in hobbies

When some long-term and intensely involved activities come to an end, a person frequently feels empty, restless, or useless. This problem comes into sharp awareness when certain time structuring activities such as caring for children, going to college, or working on a long-term project suddenly come to an end.

When a person has devoted a huge amount of time and energy into a long-term endeavor, he may create a neural network for that activity itself. If it becomes habitual it can lead to work-a-holism. In the midst of activities, different ways of being together can emerge. Rituals, pastimes, mind games, and even intimacy may occur.

Journal Exercise: How does the concept of activities as a means of structuring time play out in your life? Do you use activities in healthy ways? Unhealthy ways? Did either of your parents use activities to avoid conflict and intimacy? Do you or your partner use activities as a means of avoid conflict or intimacy? Do the amount of activities you are obligated to get in the way of your relationship?

2.2.5 Mind Games

Mind games are habitual subconscious programs of behavior that exist in the implicit memory and run subconsciously; i.e., usually beneath the awareness of even the initiator of the game. Another term for games is "survival skills"; co-created by the Little Professor and the Adapted Child ego-states in order to adapt to the dysfunction of the environment.

Psychological and Relationship Games are interpersonal time structuring options sandwiched in between the safer, more superficial option of engaging in **Pastimes** and the riskier, more candid option of authentic **Intimacy**. Psychological games were first identified and cataloged by Eric Berne MD, founder of Transactional Analysis, in his classic book from the mid-1960s, *Games People Play*. Berne defined a "game" as a patterned and predictable **series of transactions** which are superficially plausible but actually conceal motivations and lead to a well-defined predictable outcome.

A transaction is an instance of communication between two people (two players in the case of games). The initiator sends the **stimulus** and the receiver chooses a **response**. When analyzing the games we play this stimulus/response interchange is called a set of "moves"; player one makes the first move (the stimulus) and the second player responds with a move of her/her own (the response). The stimulus is an "invitation" to play a game by player one to player two. If player two responds as expected to the invitation by player one, the transaction is called complementary. The diagram below shows a ***complementary transaction***:

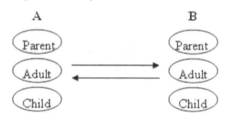

A: *What time is it?*
B: *6:30*

In this case, the complementary transaction was a simple exchange of information. The Adult ego-state is the computer part of our personality. It deals with information, data, "how-to" questions, and getting things done. It is not encumbered by emotions. Person A requested information and person B provided it. In the above diagram the communication occurred *between the same ego-state* of both parties. But complementary transactions can also occur *between different ego-states*. In the diagram below, a couple is at the mall to pick up a few things. They are on a very tight budget and things are very tough.

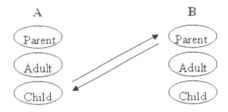

A: *Wow! This sofa is perfect, can we buy it!*
B: *Now you know we can't afford that sofa,*
   We can barely make the rent.

You can always tell a complementary transaction by the parallel lines. When two people are communicating in a complementary fashion the exchange can go on indefinitely. Partner A made a request for *permission* from Partner B which is coming from the Child ego-state; that's what kids do. So the invitation is for Partner B to come back from the Parent ego-state by either approving or denying permission, and like a Parent, cooler heads prevailed.

If Partner B would have come from an unexpected ego-state then the communication would have been "crossed." Crossed transactions usually arise out of our need to re-enact the games of our childhood. They are frequently the "Freudian slips" that initiate a psychological mind game. These games create another round of the Chemistry of Drama that becomes so familiar that we have to ask, "how in the world does this keep happening to me?"

But crossed transactions are not always a bad thing. For example, in the diagram below, once person A's invitation to play the "game" is recognized, person B can use a "cross" to short circuit the game by responding as the Adult to the Adult (in the case below, by asking a "how to" question instead of giving permission to the child or scolding the child).

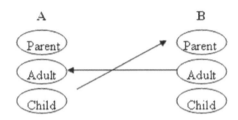

A: *Wow! This sofa is perfect, can we buy it!*
B: *If we by that sofa today how will we pay the rent tomorrow?*

Crossed transactions occur when Person A, in one ego state, addresses Person B, who is in a different ego state. As demonstrated above, some crossed transactions cause conflict and others resolve conflict. In the above diagram it is likely to have resolved the issue and ended the conversation.

You can always tell a crossed transaction because the lines of communication (?) are always crossed. We will explore using the crossed transaction to improve communication and resolve conflict in a later section on communication. For now, I just want to introduce the concept of transactions as we look at the mind games people play.

Most of us have at least an intuitive sense of when games are being played. Have you ever given a person fair warning in the beginning of a new relationship, such as, *"I don't play games"* or *"I hate game playing"* or *"I don't like Players"*? But sooner or later we find ourselves feeling as though we have just been "played."

Being totally game-free is not the goal. It is not realistic to believe that two wounded people can suddenly be able to authentic intimacy one hundred percent of the time. Neither is it wise to expect that everyone we meet will be game-free. The goal is to be able to remove harmful games from our significant relationships – that takes work and commitment by both parties. But if you want the *"happily-ever-after"* ending, this work must be done.

When we get triggered we are sure to enter into a harmful mind game that causes another cycle of abandonment, shame, and contempt to be acted out. You can always tell if you are involved in a mind game because you will notice that familiar Chemistry of Drama. We will not cover all the possibilities here (and there are many).

We don't need to cover them all because they all fit into one main format – **the Drama Triangle**. We will introduce the Drama Triangle first and then look at a few well known mind games.

2.3.1 The Drama Triangle

The Drama Triangle, created by Transactional Analyst Steven Karpman, is the game most often played game in the dysfunctional family or relationship. It takes two to three players in order to play this game; a *victim*, a *rescuer*, and a *persecutor*.

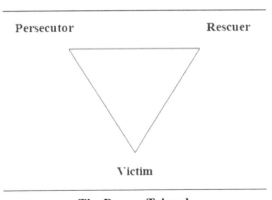

The Drama Triangle

The Victim: This player gets his needs met by having other people take care of them. Victims tend to blame others for what's wrong in their lives and play the "why don't you, yes but" game or the "I can't do that, because" game.

Victim Ego States

- Stuck in the Child ego-state, the Victim vacillates between the feelings of the Vulnerable/Needy Child and the Angry/Rebellious Child one moment expressing helplessness and hopelessness, the next throwing a temper tantrum.

- When Victims can't get someone to persecute them, they turn their own Critical Parent inward and persecute themselves. When they can get someone to persecute them, perhaps by playing a game of "Kick Me," they can feel fully justified in their Victim role.

The Rescuer: Due to an underlying fear of abandonment, the Rescuer needs to be needed and so they attach themselves to a Victim. Rescuers frequently notice that others always come to them with their problems and don't know why they do that.

The Rescuer subconsciously helps keep the Victim dependent by playing into the Victimhood –doing everything for that person rather than allowing the person to experience take care of her own problem. (?)

Rescuer Ego States

- Stuck in the Parent ego-state, the Rescuer has to be "all-about-others." This person usually spent much of his childhood care-taking or unsuccessfully trying to please a wounded parent, doing for a parent what the parent needed (role reversal).

- As an adult, the roles are switched – the Rescuer is the adult now and spends her/his time care-taking and trying to please a Projected Vulnerable Child.

- Being stuck in the Parent role, one way the Rescuer can experience his/her Vulnerable Child is to project that ego-state onto someone else with the help of the Little Professor.

- It goes something like this: The Rescuer projects his Vulnerable Child onto the person who is seen as the Victim. who then over-identifies with the Victim and feels compelled to step in to "fix" or "rescue."

- In this way the Rescuer is vicariously and compulsively trying to meet the unmet needs of his own Projected Vulnerable Child. So, ironically, compulsive care-taking of others, then, is really "all-about-me" and not the Victim at all.

- The Rescuer also spends considerable time in the Critical Parent ego-state, though not usually in an outward fashion. Instead, the Rescuer's Critical Parent sends subconscious messages of shame like this to the Victim: *"Don't worry, I know that you're incompetent and you need me to take care of you."*

- When things go wrong, the Rescuer can turn that Critical Parent on him/herself., minus the nurturing tone – *"You can't even take care of a simple little problem like that! What good are you?"*

- Rescuing is a covert Victim role when the Angry/Defiant Child protests, like this: *"Look at how I have to sacrifice and take care of everyone else!"* or *"I'm only trying to help and this is the thanks I get for it!"*

The Persecutor: Stuck in the Angry/Defiant Child ego-state this player is "all-about-me" and externalizes his contempt through shameless and blameless behavior. In the same way the Rescuer points his Critical Parent recordings inward, toward himself; the Persecutor primarily Projects his Critical Parent recordings outward, toward others, *"If all these other stupid people would do things my way the world would be a much better place!"*

Persecutor Ego States...

- Persecutors tend to disown their Vulnerable/Needy Child by subconsciously pushing it out of their individual awareness – i.e., repression. However, the Victim's Vulnerable/Needy Behavior triggers that same ego-state in the persecutor.

- The Persecutor's angry and critical responses to the Vulnerable Child in the Victim are subconscious re-enactments of how s/he drove his/her "disowned" Vulnerable Child into hiding;

- In this way, the Persecutor is projecting his/her own Vulnerable Child onto the Victim. So, again, ironically, the Persecutor is actually talking to a part of him/herself whenever they persecute.

- Another Persecutor ego-state is the intrusive Angry/Defiant Child who really believes, *"If it weren't for you I wouldn't have to act and feel this way!"* – a covert Victim role because it is an attempt to make the Victim responsible for the Persecutor's feelings and situation.

The Drama Triangle is a game that can be played with two or more people. In a *relationship between two people* the game goes something like this:

- The Victim feels and acts victimized, helpless, and needy
- The Rescuer steps in and takes over for the Victim
- The Rescuer soon resents having to do everything for the Victim
- The Rescuer then begins to blame and persecute the Victim
- The Victim then slides into the Rescuer role to rescue the new Persecutor
- The new Persecutor responds by sliding into the Victim role to be rescued

- The new Rescuer soon resents having to do everything for the new Victim
- The Rescuer then begins to blame and persecute the Victim
- Etc., etc., etc.

In a *family situation with at least three players* the Drama Triangle game goes something like this:

- A child plays the Victim
- One parent plays the Persecutor
- The other parent plays the Rescuer
- The Victim doesn't get a household chore completed
- The Persecutor blows up at the Victim for not doing his job
- The Rescuer interrupts the persecutor to protect and make excuses for the victim
- The Persecutor feels victimized by the Rescuer and begins to pout or sulk (shifting to Victim)
- The Victim rescues the Persecutor by persecuting the Rescuer (shifting to Rescuer)
- The Rescuer feels victimized and begins to persecute the original Victim (shifting to Persecutor)
- On and on it goes (negative chemistry) until there is a ceasefire (positive chemistry – relief) and the family is "doing fine" again (no chemistry) until next time when someone gets bored and initiates another round.

Journal Exercise: Examine **your current and past relationships** for a moment. Most of us shift from one role to the other, but identify with a primary role. Which role are you most familiar with in your family of origin? What role did your parents tend to play?

Which role are you most familiar with in your adult life? What role did your partners tend to play? What do you imagine your relationships and life would be like without this game?

Distorted Perceptions: The following diagram represents the distorted perceptions that occur **when a person stays stuck in one corner of the Drama Triangle.** It's like they can only see the world, and others in it, through the window behind which they are stuck.

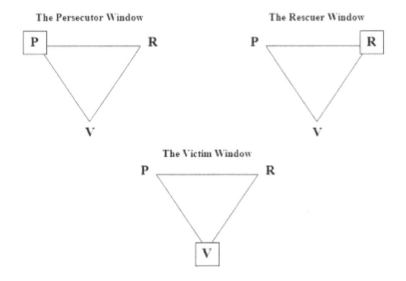

- **From behind the Persecutor Window**... Other people either look and sound like Victims or Rescuers. The Persecutor feels compelled to "set them straight."
- **From behind the Rescuer Window**... Other people either look and sound like Victims or Persecutors. The Rescuer feels compelled to intervene and save the Victim from the Persecutor(s).
- **From behind the Victim Window**... Other people either look and sound like Persecutors or Rescuers. The Victim feels compelled to relate to them as such, by getting a Rescuer to step in and fight his fight with the Persecutor which keeps them stuck in dependency on others.

Journal Exercise: Did/Does anyone in your family of origin seemingly operate from one of these distorted perceptions pretty much all of the time? Do you seem to operate from behind one of these windows most of the time? Does your partner seem stuck behind one of these windows? Give as many details and examples of your answers as you can.

2.3.2 Payoffs for Playing the Game

These psychological mind games are not played for fun. They are dysfunctional subconscious programs that have been created by our Little Professor in order to adapt to the dysfunction of our family and obtain strokes – even negative strokes are better than no strokes at all. Even though many mind games can be harmful, there is always a secondary gain, or payoff, for playing – also known as a "positive intention" in Parts Integration Therapy.

The games we play are also, at least partly, the result of the role-modeling of our parents. When we watch them play certain games over and over again with each other, we develop the network for that program (Intensity and Repetition). They become part of our Love Map. Many times our parents (subconsciously) even teach us the rules and how to play the games. These teachings are apparent in the Injunctions and Attributions we carry within us throughout life.

Here is a partial list of possible Payoffs:

- **Structure time**
- **Obtain strokes** – negative and/or positive attention as with the Chemistry of Drama (stimulation, feel alive)
- **Protect one from experiences** that are believed to cause pain – e.g., trusting others or risking intimacy
- **Maintain belief systems** in a steady-state, "I'll never really be loved!"
- **Maintain familiar emotional themes** – e.g., a steady-state of abandonment, shame, and contempt

- **Confirm and maintain Psychological Positions** – e.g., "I'm not ok...you're ok"
- **Block intimacy while receiving enough strokes to "get by"** – by the way, it takes a LOT more negative strokes to get by than positive ones
- **Make life and other people predictable**

2.3.3 Some Classic Mind Games

"Now I've Got you, you SOB!" (NIGYSOB) and "Kick Me"

In a game of NIGYSOB the player selects a partner who frequently plays "Kick Me." The NIGYSOB player is externalizing contempt and hostility while the partner who plays ""Kick Me"" internalizes it. When played by a couple, the game is usually triggered suddenly when, for various possible "reasons," the NIGYSOB player flips into a fit of rage over a perceived slight made by the Kick Me player.

The Kick Me player knows from frequent experience what the buttons are that trigger the NIGYSOB player (usually jealousy and/or rage), yet cannot seem to keep from pushing them. It genuinely seems to be an "accident" to the Kick Me player because, like all games, it's a relationship mind game played by the Child ego state at a subconscious level.

For example, The NIGYSOB player is in one of "those moods," there is silent anger and the air feels thick with tension. The Kick Me player chooses the worst moment to ask a "harmless" question such as, *"What have I done now?"* to which the NIGYSOB player flies into a thirty-minute rage about how *"Everything always has to be all about you!! I can't seem to do anything to your satisfaction!!"*

Possible Payoffs (NIGYSOB):

- **Confirmation of existential position**: *I'm okay, men/women are not okay, Men/women can't be trusted*
- **Justification for inability to control rage** and abusive behavior

- **Avoidance of personal issues causing the rage** by focusing on the other person
- **Projection of disowned aspects of self**
- **Habitual behavioral pattern to create intense stimulation** – negative strokes are familiar

Roles – Persecutor claiming to be a Victim
Ego States: Critical Parent to Child

Possible Payoffs for Kick Me:

- **Confirmation of existential position**: *"I'm not okay, men/women are not okay," "I'm not ok, you're ok."*
- **Reenactment of Parent/Child relationship from childhood** – provides stimulation and intensity
- **Initiates another game** called *"Why does this always happen to me?"*
- **Obtains negative strokes** through familiar emotional themes of childhood – abandonment, shame, contempt.

Roles – Victim
Ego States: Child to Critical Parent

"If It Weren't For You..." (IWFY)

In a game of IWFY a generally insecure or passive person subconsciously chooses a domineering partner who restricts her/his activities, usually the female partner is the one restricted. Perhaps the player selects a domineering partner because s/he does not like to take risks and try new things, such as taking up photography or going back to school.

The domineering partner's controlling nature keeps the player from getting into frightening situations, perhaps for fear of failure or fear of success. It gives the IWFY player an "out" or a way to *"save face"* and not have to take the risk.

When out with friends, the Player may play a group variation of the game called *"If it Weren't for Him..."* then her cohorts could then play a game of *"Why Don't you...yes, but..."* with her by each of them offering *"Why don't you..."* ideas which she could shoot down with a *"Yes,* (I thought of that) *But...* (It won't work because...).

By staying unaware of his or her part in the game, through the use of repression or suppression, the Player's complaints of *"If it weren't for you..."* keeps her partner feeling uneasy and gives the Player various advantages in the relationship – i.e., a "card to play" in a disagreement, etc.

Possible Payoffs for IWFY:
- **Confirmation of existential position**: "I'm okay, men/women are not okay"
- **Elimination of having to confront personal fears**
- **Allows him/her to join in the Pastime** of *"If it weren't for her/him..."* with family and friends, thereby structuring time and obtaining strokes

Roles – Primarily Victim, Sometimes Persecutor
Ego States: Child to Parent

"Courtroom"

This relationship mind game is played frequently when a couple first begins marital counseling. The therapist must refuse to get pulled into this game by redirecting the couple away from it or nothing will be resolved. In counseling or out, if this game is in play, conflicts will increase in frequency and intensity with only an occasional ceasefire. Nothing will ever be resolved and matters will only get worse.

Courtroom can be played by any number of people but is essentially a three-handed game with a Prosecutor, a Defense Attorney, and a Judge. The couple take turns prosecuting each other in front of a judge – a therapist, or a talk-show host (there's a jury in this case; i.e., the audience), or anyone else who is willing to preside over the case.

One partner starts "sharing feelings" by ripping the other partner on a whole litany of issues. When the partner does get a chance to squeeze in an explanation the Prosecutor ignores it and rips off another "count" of the offenses on the list. When it's time to let the other person "share feelings" the same pattern is repeated. Nothing ever gets resolved because the mind game never gets broken up. These exchanges can go on for so many years that the couple forgets what the original issues were.

It is very important for each partner in the relationship to be his or her own Prosecutor, Defense Attorney, and Judge. Part of a good prosecution would be the fact-gathering investigation of interviewing witnesses – in this case, your Partner. Finding out how he or she feels, thoughts, and experiences is good data for the Judge to have.

An effective marital therapist is not a Judge or referee. S/he is more helpful in the role of a coach or mediator who helps negotiate the rough spots. With this approach, conflict resolution and healing can occur.

Possible Payoffs for Courtroom:
- **Confirmation of existential position**: "I'm always wrong" expressed by the excessive need to be right – Reaction Formation
- **Projection of guilt**
- **Excused from guilt**
- **Avoidance of the real issues** – lack of intimacy for whatever reason
- **Satisfies stimulus hunger** and need for intensity
- **Acting out familiar cycles** of Abandonment, Shame, and Contempt

Roles – Victim, Persecutor, Rescuer
Ego States: Conscious/Social = Adult (This is what s/he did to me...) to Adult (This is what really happened...)
Subconscious/Psychological = Child (Pick me, take my side) to Parent (You're both right)

"See what you made me do..." (SWYMD)

In a mild form of a game of SWYMD the Player, feeling unsociable, becomes engrossed in some activity which tends to insulate him/her from people. When a family member interrupts by coming into the room or calling out to ask for something, the Player's startle response causes the hammer to slip injuring a thumb, or hitting the wrong button on the keyboard and losing the computer work, or they spilling the fuel being transferred to another container.

The Player responds to any one of the above by angrily crying out, *"See What You Made Me Do!!"* Of course it's the Player's own irritation that causes the slip or mistake. When this pattern happens only very occasionally it is not considered a game. But if it tends to *reoccur frequently* then the Player's family learns to leave the Player alone when he or she is engrossed in the game. In a more intense form, SWYMD can become a way of life rather than merely a protective mechanism. The Player may spend more and more time engrossed in work or an activity rather than relating with her/his family.

Possible Payoffs for SWYMD:

- **Confirmation of existential position**: *"I'm okay, others are not okay, not safe, not to be trusted, etc." "I am blameless"*
- **Avoidance of connectedness** and the risks associated with intimacy
- **"Justifiable" anger** offers a good excuse for avoiding sexual relations
-

Roles – Victim, Persecutor
Ego States: Child to Child

2.3.4 The Punishment/Forgiveness Cycle

Another variation of the Drama Triangle is something I call the Punishment/Forgiveness Cycle. It is a model outlining the game associated with addiction and codependency. The codependent partner plays the NIGYSOB while the alcoholic/addict plays Kick Me.

The "Doing Fine" Stage: This stage is when the addiction is inactive and things are going well.

Boredom & Fantasy Stage: In this stage boredom sets in and the person begins to fantasize ways to alleviate the discomfort of boredom – he begins to watch movies in his mind's eye as a way to feel better – the addictive behavior.

Obsession & Compulsion Stage: The fantasy becomes an obsession because "watching the movie" brings up and strengthens the feelings that go with the addictive behavior, triggering a compulsion to engage in that behavior.

Acting-Out Stage: The compulsion grows so strong it is impossible for the person to resist. So, he act-out the movie they have been watching in his mind's eye. He or she continues to act-out until they get caught.

Punishment Stage: Once caught, the person enters into the punishment stage where the significant other is upset over another transgression/broken promise.

Forgiveness Stage: In this stage, the person gets into her best behavior and works her way back into the good graces of the punisher. Once forgiveness is achieved then everything is fine again – until boredom sets in.

Stamp Collecting

Perhaps you are old enough to remember the old S&H Green stamps our parents and grandparents used to collect when they went grocery shopping. Every time they bought groceries the clerk gave them a handful of these green stamps. The stamps were pasted into a booklet and when so many booklets had been filled they could be traded in for something from the S&H catalog. There is another classic TA game called **Stamp Collecting** that is based on that same system.

If "depression" was a problem then the person would save up enough "blue" stamps (things to be sad about) and trade them in for a depressive episode. The person who had a "temper problem" would save red stamps (things to be mad about) and trade them in for an angry outburst. An "alcoholic" might save up enough yellow stamps (reasons to get drunk) to earn a good drinking binge. The idea with Stamp Collecting was that each person needed to reach a threshold where some part felt justified in having the problem.

There are literally hundreds of these games that have been "discovered" since Eric Berne first wrote his Classic *Games People Play* back in the 1960s. The good news is that they all fit into the original game of two-handed or three-handed Drama Triangle. It is best to keep things simple and see how what you are doing fits into that model.

Journal Exercise: explore the ways you and your partner play the various Drama Triangle Roles. What the opening gambit or invitation? Who makes the first move? What are the moves each player is likely to make? Which of the above classic games do you most identify with and why?

2.4 Intimacy

At a deeper level of human encounter than rituals, pastimes, games, and activities lies the potential each person has for intimacy. Intimacy is free of games and free of exploitation. It occurs in those moments of human contact that arouse such feelings as desire, tenderness, empathy, vulnerability, and affection. Intimacy combines genuine giving and receiving with the candidness of "game-free" communication.

Intimacy as a way to structure time is often frightening because it involves the risk of being vulnerable. When we are in a personal relationship it calls for emotional involvement. Our Child ego state is the part of us responsible for experiencing and sharing OUR wants, OUR needs, and OUR feelings. Being the Receiver in a healthy, intimate relationship requires the ability to experience our Child ego state; asking for what we need and receiving it is carried out by the Child ego-states.

Being the Giver in a healthy, intimate relationship requires the ability to experience our nurturing Parent ego-state. Hearing our partner ask for what he or she needs and giving it to him or her is carried out by the Parent ego-state because that is the part of us responsible for protecting and nurturing ourselves and others.

Because, in a healthy, intimate relationship, people experience their Vulnerable Child energy, many times it seems easier and safer to *pass time* or to *play games* than to risk feelings such as affection or rejection, especially if intimacy was not safe or role-modeled during childhood. If the capacity for intimacy has been unnecessarily suppressed, it can be recovered. Through activating and strengthening the Adult ego state, people can change in spite of their early life experiences.

Key Points: *The Adult ego state operates from the objective position.* Ideally, the Adult ego-state consults with the Child and the Parent ego states to DECIDE several things.

As the Receiver:
- When it's safe to express the needs and feelings of the Child

- How that expression should occur and in what context
- When it's okay to "let down the boundary" and grant someone access to that vulnerable part of self.
- How to help the Child ego-state hear and accept the word "no," – respecting and trusting the decisions, autonomy, and boundaries of a partner

As the Giver:
- How and when to respond to what is being asked by a partner
- When is it appropriate and/or healthy to give a partner what is requested?
- When is it inappropriate and/or unhealthy to give what is being asked ...for you? ...a partner? ...Your relationship?
- How to say no or set boundaries in a firm yet loving way – i.e., a way that respects and validates the needs, autonomy, and feelings of a partner

Recovering the capacity for intimacy is a major goal of healing abandonment, shame and contempt. As this healing of the False Self progresses, we become more able to share who we really are with our partner – i.e., we are able to share our True Selves with each other. This is what makes healthy intimacy authentic, enriching, and fulfilling. To get there we must be able to identify the psychological and relationship games we play with each other and how to give them up so that we can co-create a healthy, game-free relationship.

Journal Exercise: Examine your current and past relationships for a moment. Are you a Giver or a Receiver or a little of both? How often have you experienced the following with your partners: Desire, Tenderness, Empathy, Vulnerability, and Affection?

Do you feel as though you tend to choose Players or that there are a lot of Games Being Played by your partners? Have there been times when you've been a Player too? How often, and what were the games like? What other revelations have you had as you read the above material?

Section 3: Co-Creating a Healthy Relationship

In order to move from game-playing into healthy intimacy one must be able to move from survival-mode into growth-mode. These games are scripted behaviors that run automatically beneath our awareness. The next section focuses on Self-Actualization and growth. As we will see, co-creating a new relationship style requires commitment, self-awareness and work. Just a reminder: *you cannot have a healthy relationship with someone else if you do not have a healthy relationship with yourself.* Check out *Thawing Adult/Child Syndrome* if you have not already done so.

3.1 What Does a Healthy Relationship Look Like?

Dr. William Glasser, creator of Reality Therapy, identifies the healthy relationship as the foundation for good emotional and mental health.

Four Abilities Required for a Healthy Relationship:

- Give Love
- Receive Love
- Feel worthwhile to self
- Feel worthwhile to others

Externalizers or "Takers" are all-about-themselves, so they are good at receiving love and feel worthwhile to themselves, but not so good at giving love or feeling worthwhile to others.

Internalizers or "Givers" are all-about-others so they are good at giving love and feel worthwhile to others, but not so good at receiving love or feeling worthwhile to themselves.

Most of us are aware that Givers and Takers seem to find each other, as do Codependents and Alcoholics, Distancers and Pursuers, or Victims and Rescuers. As we have seen, this is because they have compatible Love Maps and radar for subconscious data that draws them together by creating "chemistry" between them.

In a healthy, intimate relationship, both parties are giving and receiving love equally and, as a result, feel worthwhile to self and the other. They take responsibility for co-creating their relationship. For example, if I refuse to open up and share my true feelings with you then we cannot have intimate communication. But if I do choose to allow myself to be open and vulnerable we can enjoy healthy intimacy – provided your response reinforces my choice to share how I feel with you.

If you, on the other hand, repeatedly respond in a hurtful way to my attempts to be open, then I soon decide it's not okay to be open. In other words, *we co-create our healthy relationship patterns through our genuine attempts to communicate and our partner's supportive and authentic responses to those attempts.*

A healthy relationship does not just happen – it's like a plant – it needs to be nourished, watered, and put out in the sunshine. If the plant is not cared for properly it will begin to show signs of stress: wilting, turning yellow – eventually it dies.

There is an old saying, "If you keep doing what you are doing, you will keep getting what you are getting." Reversing that, *"If you want something different, you must do something different."* But what is it we need to do differently? To start with, we need to accept that in reality there is no such thing as a "relationship." This word is a "nominalization." A nominalization is a verb (an action word) that has been turned into a noun (person, place or thing). You can always spot a nominalization with the wheelbarrow test – *can you put it in a wheelbarrow and cart it around?* If a relationship were a thing it would pass the wheelbarrow test. But it's not a *thing*; it is an *action* – something we do! We co-create a healthy relationship by relating to each other in certain healthy ways.

When we turn our relationship into a thing it becomes easy to lose sight of our responsibility and obligation. That's when we can say things like, *"We just grew apart."* Or, *"Things just didn't work out,"* or *"The relationship changed."* But when we see it for what it really is – a verb – then we must ask ourselves questions like, "What am I *doing* in this relationship?" "What am I *relating* to my

128

partner through my words and actions?" "How am I *relating* that?" "What can I *do* differently?"

Journal Exercise: If you are currently in a relationship, is your partner actively working through this program with you? If not, is it realistic to expect your partner to become involved in working on this with you? Why or Why not? What needs to happen for you to move forward from here as a couple?

3.1.1 Traits of a Healthy Relationship:

Below is a list of eight more nominalizations that will give us some important clues to what we need to do to co-create a healthy relationship:

1. Love – The two toughest questions of existence – "What is life?" and "What is love?" I do not claim to know the answers to these questions because I feel it's something highly subjective and personal. We all have to answer these questions for ourselves and we all have our own constantly evolving cognitive map for the terms. Whatever "true love" means to you is going to guide all of your action, reactions, and decisions in the arena of relationship because it is so closely tied to the pain and pleasure continuum.

There is nothing quite like "getting it right" in a healthy relationship, and nothing quite like "getting it wrong" and losing at love. To me, sports are the closest I can get to something similar. I'm old enough to remember the old *ABC Wide World of Sports* tagline – *"...the thrill of victory and the agony of defeat!"* Whatever love means to YOU, it must be there for you to stay motivated to last the entire season and "win the Superbowl."

We know now that love is a verb – an action word. It's not a "thing" that exists between us. It's *something we demonstrate over and over again in our actions and reactions*. Love is a behavior that helps us co-create a loving, healthy relationship. Like the term "relationship," "love" is a nominalization. We must turn both terms back into action words in order to "get it right."

The action word for relationship is to "relate." When we step back and ask *How is our relationship going?* it's the wrong question. We need to get specific and ask questions like:

- Who is doing most of the relating?
- Who is relating what to whom?
- Am I relating what I want to relate to my partner?

Many times people miss the expressions of love by their partners because they are looking for the wrong things. Some expect to hear frequent "I Love You's"... But their partners may have learned to express love by some other method such as:

- Working hard to make a comfortable living
- Giving gifts
- Spending time together
- Affectionate touch
- Doing things for their partner

It is important to be able to ask for what you need. In fact, the hallmark of a dysfunctional relationship is that it is NOT okay to ask directly for what you need. Perhaps you have repeatedly asked your partner for more physical affection. The partner may try for a few days but then things "go back to normal." It's usually because your partner does not have that particular behavior built into his/her neural network for love, also known as a Love Map.

In this case, your partner must "practice" by consciously making an effort to give you what you need. At first it will feel solicited (because it is) but within a few weeks can become automatic and unsolicited; a part of your synchronized map for how you do love as a couple.

It's much easier to run on auto-pilot and go with our subconscious programming than it is to develop new programming with conscious effort. All those New Year's resolutions that we fail to keep are examples of this. However, for something as important as your healthy relationship, it's wise to invest the effort in updating your Love Map. Maybe just one thing at a time, but do it whenever possible.

There is a presupposition in NLP that states, *"You cannot NOT communicate."* It means that your very lack of relating is relating something to your partner. The remainder of this list contains other nominalized traits worth relating to each other that will help you "get it right" – *provided you really want to invest in and co-create a healthy relationship.*

2. Mutuality – Mutuality is a blend of acceptance and equality where partners in a healthy relationship demonstrate the following actions:

- Accept each other as they are
- Make sure each of their needs are given equal priority
- Are willing to make sacrifices for win-win scenarios
- Encourage and support each other in pursuit of individual goals and dreams, even if that means less time together. In some cases – even if it means letting them go by mutually ending or suspending the relationship.

3. Intimacy – True intimacy is the ability to share who you really are with another person. This presupposes that you have a partner who is also willing and able to share who they really are with you. If you've read the Iceberg Model in the beginning chapters of this book then you know about the Invented-Self, the False-Self, and the True-Self; sharing your **True Self** demands that you have access to that part of you.

Those who have been affected by the woundedness of others may not know who they really are – Some may even have Adult/Child Syndrome, Codependency, Addiction, Depression, or some other chronic condition that limits or impairs their ability to share who they really are. If this is true in your case (as it is with most of us) then your healthy relationship can only come with a plan for healing your own woundedness as a first step.

To gain self-awareness and healing it is important to go back and complete *Thawing Adult/Child Syndrome*, or counseling, or join an Adult/Child Group, or do all of these. If you already have self-awareness (i.e., you know your issues and are doing something about them) then you may be ready for the work of co-creating your future. Even in the best of circumstances laying the groundwork for a healthy relationship is hard work. But with a great payoff!

A word about sex – Healthy couples have a great sex life because they have discovered that sex is the "gravy on top" and that the "meat and potatoes" of their partnership is the intimacy that comes from the emotional connection that they share. Some people place so much emphasis on sex that they don't feel inclined to do the work of building a healthy relationship.

While sex is an intimate act and as close as two people can *physically* get to one another... it's just not the same without having the emotional connection that comes from true intimacy – sharing who you really are. This issue alone is frequently why many relationships fail. You cannot survive for long on gravy alone. I'll go out on another limb here and say that you have never experienced great sex if you have not first connected fully on an emotional level.

4. Response-able Partners – Response-able partners accept that they have the ability-to-respond in any way they choose to any situation in their life. They refuse to put on the mantle of Victimhood which is handed out so easily in our culture. They refuse to play the same old mind games that they grew up with.

They may have irrational thoughts, limiting beliefs, emotional wounds, and other issues in their life that hold them back – but they are doing something about it. They know that they can change and are actively involved in personal growth. (More on Response-ability later)

5. Trust & Safety – Trust & Safety cannot be separated. They are the byproducts of practicing the ideas and behaviors list here. Have you ever tried to pull a blanket off of someone who is cold? They just hold on that much tighter. If you want them to take the blanket off, then turn up the emotional thermostat to "warm and safe" and they will take it off themselves. (Melody Beattie, *The Language of Letting Go*, p.249)

6. Adaptability – People in a healthy relationship are flexible and can adapt to the changing needs of their partner. They value differentness as much as they do sameness. They can agree to disagree without it affecting the way they relate to each other.

7. Commitment – All of the above takes supreme effort and commitment. The first item on this list (Love) will provide the motivation and energy to stick with this last item – a strong commitment to tighten the "nuts and bolts" in between.

Journal Exercise: Examine your current and past relationships for a moment. Which of the above seven traits are your assets? Which are your liabilities? Where do you need to begin in order to build your relationship? Who needs to do what? What do you need? Other thoughts and observations?

3.2 What Does a Toxic Relationship Look Like?

Okay, so now you know what a healthy relationship looks like. So let's take a look at the state of your current relationship. Don't worry, this is not an either-or proposition. Even the worst relationships have a bit of good in them and even the best relationships have a bit of bad in them. Most relationships fall somewhere in between those two poles. Let's begin by looking at some signs of problems in a relationship.

3.2.1 Twenty Signs of Relationship Problems

These twenty signs of marital and relationship problems are another way to evaluate the current health of your relationship. Compare these with the traits of a healthy relationship above to get a clear picture of the problems. They are partially adapted from John Bradshaw's excellent ten-hour workshop on compact disc, *Post Romantic Stress Disorder*. The reader can order the program and many of his other books, CDs and DVDs at www.johnbradshaw.com.

1. Slowly accelerating and repetitive conflicts... *without effective resolution*:

Top Three Marital Conflicts...

- **Over the Control of money**...*without effective resolution*
- **Over the Frequency of sex**... *without effective resolution*
- **Over Family matters**... *without effective resolution*

Notice that it's not the conflict, but the lack of resolution that is the problem.

2. Accelerating power struggles with each partner believing they are better, and/or more "right" than their mate. Skirmishes continue with occasional major battles and cease fires.

- **Score keeping** – Attacking and criticizing each other's contributions to the relationship...keeps the focus on the problem frame vs. the solution frame.
- **Attacking and criticizing** each other's differences causing self-generating cycles of abandonment, shame, and contempt.

3. Withdrawal/Isolation – Bradshaw's *Four Horsemen of the marital Apocalypse* – more cycles of abandonment, shame and contempt.

- Criticizing leads to attacking
- Attacking to shame
- Shame to withdrawal
- Withdrawal to isolation

Treating each other like an enemy can only end in with surrender or a temporary ceasefire. Your partner is supposed to be your best friend. When you treat your partner like an enemy they are likely to react like one by defending, attacking, or withdrawing.

4. Hypersensitivity – When relationship problems are ongoing they becomes second nature, dropping into the subconscious mind as an implicit memory network – i.e., it becomes an automatic subconscious program and the defenses stay up for self-protection.

When we get good at something it means that the neural network for that behavior has grown. The human brain is compelled to continue to grow. So, we get better at everything we practice regularly.

KEY POINT: Remember the two methods for creating and developing a neural network are intensity and repetition. Unresolved conflicts tend to become increasingly intense and repetitive. At some point fighting becomes the habitual way of relating to each other – ***the Steady State.***

5. Misinterpretation – hypersensitivity and defensiveness leads to distortions in sending and receiving messages – i.e., communication breaks down and para-messages send signals of war.

6. Original emotional wounds get worse from ongoing shaming (name calling and belittling) and abandonment (Threats of abandonment and walking out)...hurting the ones we love the most.

7. Immediately wanting to escape and flee the relationship - more abandonment – Escape comes in many forms...*TV, drinking, shopping, working, etc.*

8. Bonded together by the "Terror of Aloneness" – We come back to, or stay in an unhappy relationship to avoid being alone – the Inner Child fear of abandonment – children can't leave

9. The relationship is enmeshed, then disengaged – more abandonment and painful, "make-up/break-up" cycles of connectedness and separateness

10. Each partner is deficient in emotional literacy – unable to process feelings in a healthy way, they just give up trying and numb-out emotionally.

- Without emotion nothing matters
- With emotion everything matters

11. Unmet childhood dependency needs – Spontaneous age regression is triggered causing childlike feelings and behaviors, e.g., Adult/Child Syndrome.

When we get married unmet childhood dependency needs emerge. One might be CEO of the company during the day and throw child-like temper tantrums at home in the evenings. The dominant brain is where the CEO resides; non-dominant brain is where the Angry/Defiant and Vulnerable/Needy Child ego-states reside, i.e., the subconscious mind.

If your initial secure attachment was to a wounded parent, you will carry their feelings (rage, shame, depression) in your attachment to them, as if there were an emotional umbilical cord. Feelings work is a must. Original pain must be surfaced and released, grief process must begin, and emotional separation from the unhealthy parental attachment must occur.

12. Differences are treated as threats – Boundary issues, don't think what you thin…think what I think!

13. Triangulation occurs: for example, extramarital affairs or pulling a child into the relationship in order to avoid intimacy, the Dance of Externalization

14. A history of Cross-generational bonding is present: a child becomes the special one, sorority sister, surrogate spouse, daddy's girl, mama's boy, little princess, etc.

Cross-generational bonding occurs whenever there is an alliance that forms between one parent and child against the other parent... The child subconsciously feels *"I'm more important than the other parent to this parent."* This sets up the Drama Triangle

15. Avoiding one's partner by engaging in an addiction... includes working or playing excessively at the exclusion of the other...diversion of energy into other things that bring illusion of relief – survival skills

16. Accelerating disdain of partner which leads to re-definition of the whole relationship

17. Lack of shared interests or time together to be involved with each other

18. Loss of awareness for the needs of the partner

19. Lack of concern for the needs of the partner

20. Inability to know/express our own needs...lose touch with True-Self

Journal Exercise: Examine your current and past relationships for a moment. Which of these signs are you familiar with in your current and past relationships? List everything you see as a significant issue.

3.2.2 Are You "Living Life in Reaction?"

We all possess a natural instinct for survival. It's often referred to as the stress response or *the "Fight-Flight-or-Freeze" response.*

Imagine you are walking through the woods and you suddenly hear a rustling of the leaves; you "freeze" for a moment and look around, really tuning into the space around you. Then you see it. And it sees you – a small squirrel freezes for a moment, evaluates the situation and then runs away (flight response). Now, if "it" was a grizzly bear, you'd be the one taking flight (unless you were calm, cool, and collected enough to over-ride your natural response and try the playing dead approach).

Now imagine that you chase that squirrel, get him into a corner with no escape, then reach in to pick him up. That's right; you would witness first-hand the transformation of a harmless squirrel into a miniature grizzly bear (fight response). And if it was the Grizzly reaching in to get you, it's not likely that you would go quietly without a fight either.

These instinctive responses are hard-wired into the brain in order to ensure the survival of all living things. We don't have to remember to do them, or learn to do them, or consider doing them, or wonder if it's time to do them – fortunately, they come to us naturally and instantly. Out of this natural instinct comes the excessive need for control which is the catalyst for all codependent and counter-dependent behavioral patterns.

The Dysfunctional Family as a "Battleground"

Whenever there is a perceived threat or danger, alarms go off in the brain and the Fight-Flight-or-Freeze response gets triggered. When triggered, we may freeze for just a moment to take in enough data for a split-second evaluation, and then react. It has been said by most experts that Codependents "live life in reaction" – they simply react and rarely can they tell you why they did. This reactivity would be consistent with the hyper-vigilance developed by wounded children who live in an emotionally or physically unsafe environment such as a dysfunctional family.

When stress hits (money trouble, marital discord, drinking binges, broken promises, etc.); that's when the functioning of the family is more likely to become impaired because this survival instinct gets triggered when there is a perceived threat.

For moderate-to-severely dysfunctional families it is at high-stress periods that cycles of abandonment, shame, and contempt are most active between members of the family. These are the times that emotional injuries result. They can be very chaotic, emotionally threatening and/or dangerous times for everyone – *the family environment then becomes a battleground.*

Friend or Enemy?

On a battleground, the survival instinct takes over and fight-or-flight reflexes are triggered. When that happens, *family members begin to treat each other like enemies. There are three ways to treat someone like an enemy*: **attack** (fight), **defend** your position (fight), or *physically and/or emotionally* **retreat** (flight). When someone treats you like an enemy in one of those ways, what is your instinctive response? That's right, you are instinctively going to feel obliged to counter-attack, defend, or retreat which is treating them like an enemy. Your natural instinct for survival takes over and you just react. This is how we end up *"living life in reaction."*

It should be noted here that many small children in a dysfunctional family cannot fight back, are not able or allowed to defend themselves, and many times cannot even physically retreat – *they are trapped as if they were prisoners of war (POW's).* The only defenses left to them are to emotionally retreat and/or escape into fantasy. Their *Little Professor* helps by repressing their overwhelming emotions and creating ways to survive as a POW – such as *people-pleasing, compliance, perfectionism, stifling their own needs and instincts,* etc.

These children, raised by Angry/Defiant & Critical parents who have disowned their Vulnerable/Needy Child energy, were not allowed to express anger or have their own opinion. Many times they were not even allowed to express any neediness or vulnerability because it would trigger the same in their Externalizing parent who would then attack and criticize them for being "weak."

But some kids, raised by Vulnerable/Needy wounded parents who have disowned their own Angry/Defiant energy, are allowed to run roughshod over others because their parents cannot set healthy boundaries. These kids are reinforced for externalization of their abandonment, shame, and contempt.

Even more confusing to children is when they have both types of parents; one who is a rigid Externalizer and the other who is a Vulnerable/Needy Internalizer of abandonment, shame, and contempt.

An occasional argument or disagreement does not constitute a battleground. However, repetitive or intense, angry eruptions with the use of verbal and/or physical weapons such as threats of abandonment, shaming behavior (name-calling, belittling, and/or discounting), and other forms of verbal or physical abuse does constitute a battleground and/or POW camp – and in some cases an outright war zone!

Sometimes the battle is more subtle – a covert operation if you will. There may be silent anger, non-verbal forms of shaming and discounting (eye-rolling, hostile looks, etc.), withdrawal of love or affection, emotional or physical absence (work addictions), and secret assaults on the family such as extra-marital affairs. Even though there may be a façade of calmness on the surface of things, the emotional atmosphere can be very thick or cloudy and the injuries can run just a deep.

In a family, we are not supposed to treat each other like enemies. Husbands and wives are supposed to be best friends who love, honor and trust each other. Moms and Dads are supposed to be all about the welfare of the children – protecting, nurturing and providing for them. In a dysfunctional family, these things don't happen consistently enough, if at all. Any kind of repetitive and/or intense battles that have no resolution and simply end in a cease-fire constitutes a battleground.

Regardless if the dysfunction is mild, moderate, or severe; "walking wounded" are always the result. How wounded is the only remaining question. In moderate-to-severely dysfunctional families Post-Traumatic Stress Disorder (PTSD) – what was originally known as *Combat Fatigue* because it was an emotional wounding first noticed in soldiers returning from the battleground – can be the result.

Learning to protect one's self from emotional and sometimes physical injury requires creativity and the ability to adapt to *the family dance.* The Drama Triangle, the Punishment/Forgiveness Cycle, and Distance & Pursuit are three such family dances. These wargames follow us into our adulthood and relationships.

Journal Exercise: How does the above discussion on survival-mode, wargames, and your family of origin pertain to you and your life? Do you feel trapped in survival-mode in your current relationship? Do you feel your relationship is growing? If yes, how did you accomplish that? If no, how do you and your partner "act like enemies" toward one another?

3.2.3 First Things First

We cannot heal the pain of a whole lifetime all at once – we must take care of *first-things-first.* In order to be in position to co-create a healthy relationship we must start at the tip of the Iceberg and work our way down. *This means first transitioning out of, and stabilizing from any addictions or other self-destructive methods of distraction from inner pain*; methods such as obsessions, compulsions, emotional numbing, and chronic worry to name a few.

Some people are not able to relate to a childhood of moderate or severe abandonment, yet they find themselves in a very chaotic relationship with a significant other or a family member that is addicted to alcohol, drugs, gambling, work, drama, etc. Or someone who has some condition that they appear to be using as an excuse to become a helpless victim such as diabetes, chronic or treatment-resistant depression, an anxiety problem or some other condition for which they DO NOT take responsibility for managing – like the diabetic who has sugar stashes and binges, or someone who has Bipolar Disorder but frequently goes off their meds, or someone who has ADHD but refuses to do the things necessary to manage their condition.

In cases like these one can get pulled into a trap where they assume responsibility for their loved one. In the Enabling game, these rescuers progressively experience cycles of abandonment, shame, and contempt in their relationship with the "victim" so that what was a mild case of family dysfunction in childhood becomes worse and grows into a moderate-to-severe case of original pain. The more out-of-control things get in the relationship, the more the enabling partner assumes control and ends up enmeshed in the problem with no apparent way out – so they begin to act and feel as if they were a martyr – which is an advanced form of the Rescuer role in the Drama Triangle.

The Enabling Trap

Enabling behavior is born of our instinct for love. It's only natural to want to help someone we love, but when it comes to certain problems helping is like throwing a match on a pool of gasoline. In the true sense of the word, to enable is to supply with the means, knowledge, or opportunity to be or do something – to make feasible or possible. In its true form, then, "enabling" means something positive. It's our natural instinct to reach out and help someone we love when they are down or having problems.

However, when we apply it to certain problems in living, such as addictions, chronic financial trouble, codependency, and the other issues mentioned above, enabling behaviors have the reverse effect of what is intended. As the problem gets more out-of-control the more codependent experiences the excessive need to control.

Below are some examples of enabling behaviors. Most of these are "Rescuer" behaviors from the Drama Triangle:

- Repeatedly bailing them out – of jail, financial problems, other "tight spots" they get themselves into
- Giving them "one more chance" ...then another...and another
- Ignoring the problem - because they get defensive when you bring it up or your hope that it will magically go away
- Joining them in the behavior when you know they have a problem with it - Drinking, gambling, etc.,
- Joining them in blaming others – for their own feelings, problems, and misfortunes
- Accepting their justifications, excuses and rationalizations – "I'm destroying myself with alcohol because I'm depressed."
- Avoiding confronting the problem – "keeping the peace," believing a lack of conflict will help
- Doing for them what they should be able to do for themselves
- Softening or removing the natural consequences of the problem behavior
- Trying to "fix" them or their problem
- Repeatedly coming to the "Rescue"
- Trying to control them or their problem

As already mentioned, one can grow up in a family with mild dysfunction, attach to a problem person, and fall into the enabling trap thereby worsening their once mild abandonment and shame issues in their adult years. But for the codependent person who did grow up with moderate-to-severe childhood abandonment issues, enabling in their most significant relationships is almost a sure thing.

In Section 1.5 on pp. 84-86 we discussed dysfunctional relationships resulting from Infatuation & Identification vs. authentic Intimacy. If you or your partner has an active, untreated addiction it takes your relationship to a whole other level of dysfunction! The diagram below depicts two people relating to each other through the *Insanity of Addiction* and codependency, complicating the other three alternatives even further:

Cycles of Abandonment, Shame, & Contempt

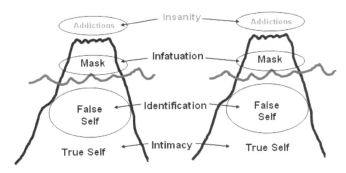

Journal Exercise: How does the above information relate to you? Have you ever enabled a partner? Have you ever been enabled? If so, write about that here. Also explore details about any relationships that included living with addiction and codependency.

3.2.4 Signs of Addiction

How does one determine if they have an addiction? The easiest way to find out is to turn your focus inward and just ask yourself this question: *"Do I continue to seek comfort or relief through some object or activity even though it causes serious negative consequences in me or my life?"* Then just listen to your intuition for that "still small voice" from within. (Maybe it's not so small and maybe it's kind of loud!) Either way, if you get a "yes" response then explore the following signs and symptoms of addiction to see if some of them fit for you. Remember to look for the similarities and ignore the differences (not the other way around).

Early Stage of Addiction

- **Relief Using** – drinking, comfort eating, spending, working, etc.
- **Increase in Tolerance** – for the amount or frequency of use or for the behavior
- **Preoccupation** – with the object or event (people are objects in addiction and codependency)
- **Loss of Control** – over type, amount, frequency; over emotions or behavior (Excessive eating, yelling at the kids)
- **Continued Use** (of object, event or enabling behavior) Despite Serious Negative Consequences

Middle or "Crucial" Stage of Addiction

- **Family Problems** - Drama Triangle and/or the Punishment/Forgiveness Cycle (see above)
- **Social Problems** – Embarrassing self or others, losing friends, avoiding parties and gatherings because of the object or activity.
- **Emotional Problems** – Depression, anxiety, chronic stress
- **Financial Problems**
- **Legal Problems** – Domestic disturbances, DWI/DUI, other
- **Occupational or Academic Problems** – Loss of concentration due to preoccupation with the problem or problems person(s)

Late or "Chronic" Stage of Addiction

- **Physical Deterioration** – headaches, stomach problems, stress disorders, problems with the liver, pancreas, ulcer, etc.
- **Serious Physical Withdrawal Syndrome** – cannot stay away after a break-up or separation from object or event
- **Obsession** - preoccupation increases until it takes the majority of your thoughts

- **Loss of Social Supports** – stop seeing friends and begin to isolate, other people give up trying to get you to see what you are doing, people drop you or drift away
- **Collapse of the Alibi System** – can no longer make excuses for yourself OR the problem or problem person(s)
- **Drinking, Using Prescription Meds, Eating, Working**, etc. to keep functioning or "feel normal"
- **Hopelessness and Despair**
- **Untimely Death** – accident, suicide, illnesses secondary to the addiction/codependency

Just one of these symptoms is not enough in-and-of themselves to identify an addiction. However, if you find you can agree with even a few of the items on the list then there is an index of suspicion that you are in an addictive process. The more items you identify with the higher that index of suspicion goes. A visit to a professional addiction specialist is in order if there is any index of suspicion at all. You cannot change anything unless you treat and stabilize an active addiction. Especially drugs, alcohol, gambling, sex, porn, video games, work-a-holism, and eating disorders.

Any attempts to deal with the pain of the past will trigger cravings to seek comfort and relief in the only way you know how – your addiction of choice. It is sometimes necessary to take as much as a year of two to get well adjusted to a recovery program before taking on emotional and interpersonal problems.

As the chart below indicates, the earlier you identify an addictive process the easier it is to arrest and stabilize that process and make healthy changes for recovery.

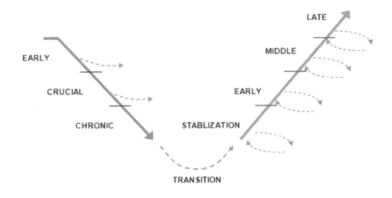

Key:

$\longrightarrow$ Disease Process

$-\ -\ -\ -\to$ Point of Intervention (Recovery can happen at any point in the disease process)

$\longrightarrow$ Recovery Process

$-\ -\ -\ -\to$ Relapse Process (Relapse can happen at any point in the recovery process)

3.2.5 Signs of Codependency

Codependency is an "addiction to the outside" of one's self. The codependent needs something to keep their focus directed outward as a problem person such as an alcoholic or addict is the perfect external focus. The chart above is also applicable to the disease of codependency. For another way to see why codependency is considered to be an addiction, take a look at how *the signs of addiction* match *the signs of codependency*:

Early Stage of Codependency
- **Relief Using** – Comfort eating, spending, working, enabling someone (anyone) with their problem in order to avoid an internal focus.
- **Increase in Tolerance** – for the behaviors of the problem person.
- **Preoccupation** – with how to control the problem and the person
- **Loss of Control** – over emotions/behavior (excessive eating, yelling at the kids)
- **Continued Use** (of enabling behavior) Despite Serious Negative Consequences – to yourself as well as them

146

Middle Stage of Codependency

- **Family Problems** – Drama Triangle and/or the Punishment/Forgiveness Cycle
- **Social Problems** – Embarrassment, avoiding parties where they may be "too much temptation" for your partner.
- **Emotional Problems** – Depression, anxiety, chronic stress
- **Financial Problems**
- **Legal Problems** – Domestic disturbances
- **Occupational or Academic Problems** – Loss of concentration due to preoccupation with the problem person or persons

Late or "Chronic" Stage of Codependency

- **Physical Deterioration** – headaches, stomach problems, stress disorders, etc.
- **Serious Physical Withdrawal Syndrome** - cannot stay away after a break-up or separation
- **Obsession** – preoccupation increases until it takes the majority of your thoughts
- **Loss of Social Supports** – stop seeing friends and begin to isolate, other people give up trying to get you to see what you are doing
- **Collapse of the Alibi System** – can no longer make excuses for yourself OR the problem person
- **Drinking, Using Prescription Meds, Eating, Working**, etc. to keep functioning or "feel normal"
- **Hopelessness and Despair**
- **Untimely Death** – accident, suicide, illnesses secondary to the codependency

Advanced skills in the Drama Triangle and Punishment/Forgiveness games are two very common, almost universal examples of codependent behavior patterns that involve control as a primary survival-mode behavior. Remember that to lose one's external focus means that their attention would begin to drift inward – something that is to be avoided at all costs because the inner pain would surface and be fully experienced.

Journal Exercise: How does the above information relate to you? Do you have any of the signs of addiction or codependency? If so, identify them and give some examples below.

As you can see from this comparison, the symptoms of addiction and codependency are almost identical. This is because codependency IS an ADDICTION.

Just one of these symptoms is not enough in-and-of themselves to identify a Codependency. However, if you find you can agree with even a few of the items on the list then there is an index of suspicion that you are in an addictive process. The more items you identify with the higher that index of suspicion goes.

A visit to a professional addiction specialist is in order if there is any index of suspicion at all. You cannot heal the inner pain without addressing the addiction of codependency. You may also want to take a close look to see if other, secondary addictions are present. You cannot make progress if there is an active addiction, even a secondary one to prescription drugs, alcohol, food, gambling, sex, porn, video games, work-a-holism, and eating disorders.

Once these issues have been assessed and stabilized or ruled-out as a possibility, it is time then to move forward with co-creation of a healthy relationship. The remained of this book will be devoted to providing tools and recommendations to that end. The first and most important tool to explore is communication.

3.3 Communication

As we discussed earlier, there is no such thing as a "relationship" because that word is a nominalization (p.102). In reality, *there is only whatever we co-create through how we relate to each other.* Communication is another one of those nominalizations – a verb turned into a noun. It doesn't pass the wheelbarrow test either so it is "something we do" that has been magically transformed into a "thing" that occurs between us all by itself.

To communicate is to relate. We communicate through our words, our actions, our non-verbal expressions, our gestures, our writing, and our very presence. In Neuro-Linguistic Programming (NLP), thy have a saying; *"We cannot NOT communicate"*. Everything we do or don't do communicates something. Even if we sit quietly in our chair not saying anything to our partner, not looking at them, not even acknowledging their presence, it communicates something. The question is do these actions communicate what we want them to communicate?

They also have another saying in NLP, *"The meaning of my communication is in the response that I get"*. This is a reminder of our personal responsibility to make sure we send the message that we want to send. If I get a response that I don't want I can say it's your fault because you got it wrong. But blame never solved anything, it only creates unnecessary conflicts.

If I don't get the response I want the first time then I make some adjustments and try again. I keep doing that until I am sure that you received the message I wanted to send. Notice that I am not saying that I keep trying until I get you to do what I want you to do. I keep trying until I can be sure that you got the full message I intended for you to get. What you do in response to that message is, of course, up to you.

Communicating is a very sophisticated but sloppy process. We have six ways to experience "reality". We have our five senses; visual, auditory, kinesthetic (touch/feel), gustatory (taste) and olfactory (smell). And we have our native language (words). In our minds we re-present reality to ourselves in the form of "mental movies". The theatre of our mind has a soundtrack, touch track, visual track, taste track, and smell track – instead of 3D; we have a 5D movie theater!

Now here's the tricky part. In order to communicate our "reality" to another human being we must encode as many dimensions of the mind movie we want to convey *into words and non-verbal's such as tone of voice, gestures, facial expressions, etc. and then send it through the air to our partner.* Next we can only hope that our partner uses a *decoder* that is compatible with our *encoder* because they have to decode the message and play it all in the theater of their mind. And what do you think are the chances that we get it right the first time?

The margin of error in new relationships is very high. It takes time and practice to "get to know" our partner because it take time and practice to synchronize our communication devices. But how many couples do you know who have been together so long that they can finish each other's sentences – and still enjoy talking to each other! Once we "get on the same wavelength" we can more easily communicate with each other. The longer we are in that relationship the easier it gets to communicate.

So then how does it happen that two people who have been together for a long time suddenly realize they don't really know each other anymore? Or they have just "grown apart"? Assuming they were able to genuinely communicate earlier in their relationship, it is obvious that somewhere along the line they quit communicating, or never really wanted to, and were satisfied with that arrangement for a time. If two people stop communicating with each other they are relating disinterest and abandoning their "relationship." Sooner or later that kills their relationship – the plant dies for lack of water and sunshine.

And what of those who just cannot seem to stop fighting all the time? This is often referred to as a "breakdown in communication." Couples like this will often say, *"We just can't communicate."* That is obviously not true, because fighting is communicating. The question is, *what is the fighting communicating?* Usually constant conflict results when a couple has reached an impasse and neither of them is getting what they want or need. So they just keep fighting to make each other pay by communicating messages of abandonment, shame, and contempt. This, too, eventually kills or seriously injures the relationship by perpetuating the original pain of abandonment.

Journal Exercise: Describe any communication problems you tend to experience in your current and past relationships and give some examples below.

3.3.1 Ego-State Functioning in Communication

In *Thawing Adult/Child Syndrome* we learned about ego-states as they relate to *intra-personal functioning*. We used a ***Structural Ego-State Map*** like the one below in that case. This structural map shows the structure of our personality:

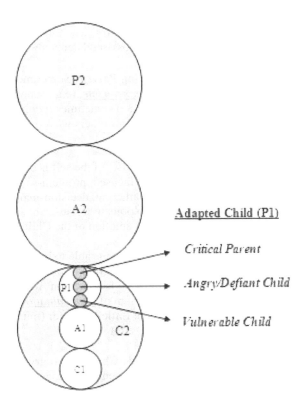

For our purposes here we need an ego-state map that we can use to explore the *functions* of ego-states in our communication. The diagram below is a ***Functional Ego-State Map***. This map allows us to explore the *interpersonal dynamics* of our ego-states in the process of communicating with another person.

Functional Ego-State Map:

CP = Controlling Parent; sometimes it is *appropriate* to take control (e.g., when suicidal, committing one to hospital) other times it is *inappropriate* control (e.g., interfering in their relationships, bossy and demanding)

NP = Nurturing Parent; Sometimes being nurturing is *appropriate*, (e.g., supportive after the loss of loved one) sometimes *inappropriate* (fixing, rescuing, doing for others what they should be doing for themselves)

Adult = The "CEO of the self is clear thinking, here-and-now focused, problem-solving, information gathering, decision-making ego-state with access to objective, cause and effect thinking undistorted by emotion of the Child ego-states.

The Adult ego-state is able to borrow creativity and imagination of the Little Professor; but when distorted thinking is present in Adult decision-making, it's a sign of *contamination* by the magical thinking of the Little Professor (mind-reading, personalizing, etc.)

AC = Adapted Child; The Vulnerable/Needy Child and Angry/Defiant Child energies that *inappropriately* act-out abandonment, shame, and contempt when triggered. Sometimes it is *appropriate* to access/express our angry and defiant energy (to say "no") or vulnerable and needy energy (for authentic Intimacy).

FC = Free Child; *Appropriate* and *inappropriate* (not polite to belch in a restaurant) expressions of the fun-loving, adventuresome, Natural Child energy and creative, intuitive, and manipulative Little Professor part of our personality.

We can use the Functional Ego-State Map to analyze our transactions to improve how we communicate with one another. In fact, this model is the best tool I have ever seen for learning to be an expert communicator. It can help not only in our personal relationships, but also in our professional relationships; especially if you are a manager and need to be a master at communicating effectively.

For example, let's analyze a dysfunctional interaction (*see pp. 114-116 for more information on transactions*). In the example below, Person A has been given a very important job by person B, to pick up the dry cleaning so person B has nice clothes for an important engagement this evening. Person A has already forgotten to pick it up once this week.

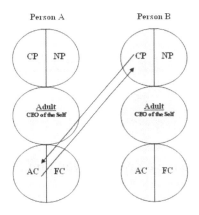

A: Please don't be upset with me, I forgot to pick up the dry cleaning again.
B: I knew I shouldn't have trusted you, you never do anything right!
A: I'm sorry! I didn't mean to upset you.
B: Oh that's a crock! You wouldn't screw things up if you really meant that!!

As long as the transactions remain complementary (p.116) this conversation can go on indefinitely. "Forgetting" again to pick up the clothes along with the opening comment by person A's Adapted Child was an invitation to person B to play the Persecutor in a game of Kick Me (p.124). The Controlling Parent comment of person B was an acceptance of the invitation, making person A the Victim of a complementary NIGYSOB move (p.124).

In order to avoid the game altogether, person B would need to make an unexpected move by crossing the transaction. Remember that complementary transactions are complementary because they follow a predictable course (parallel lines) – the invitation is made to a certain ego-state in the other person; if the invitation is accepted the game is on. If not accepted and person B responds from an unexpected ego-state (crossing lines) the whole thing could be avoided. Below is an example of a ***crossed transaction***:

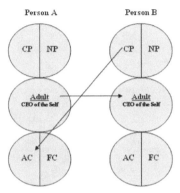

B: If I ask you to do me a favor, do you think you can do it without screwing up?
A: No.

In the above example, Person B comes from the Controlling Parent to invite an angry or wounded Child response from person A's Adapted Child. Person A declines the invitation by simply saying "No" from their Adult ego-state. Person B is left to interpret what part of the invitation was declined; was it *"...can you do me a favor"* or *"...without screwing it up?"* Person B may decide to make more invitations, give up, or rephrase the question in a more respectful way. The goal of Person A is to stay in the logical Adult ego-state by simply providing information. Another way to avoid the invitation to come from the Adapted Child is to mirror the move of the initiator as in the example below:

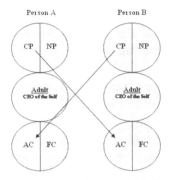

B: If I ask you to do me a favor do you think you can do it without screwing up?

A: I am not inclined to do anything at all for you when you take that tone with me.

Here person A tries to beat person B at his own game. It is unexpected and, as such, qualifies as a crossed transaction. There is a chance that person B may respond from their Adapted Child or Controlling Parent or shift back to Adult ego-State. Crossing from Adult to Adult offers the best chance of ending a dysfunctional conversation. The next best thing would be an attempt to diffuse the situation by crossing from the playful Free Child to Free Child as depicted below:

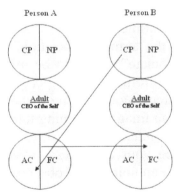

B: If I ask you to do me a favor do you think you can do it without screwing up?

A: "Oh goodie! I'd love an opportunity to screw up favor for you!"

The risk here is that the attempt to diffuse could backfire if person B is not in the mood for it and actually escalate the dysfunction if person B takes a Controlling Parent stance that you are being passive-aggressive or disrespectful (even though that would be "calling the kettle black").

With these tools you have a system for analyzing any transactions that occur and choose better ways of communicating. A couple who is serious about improving communications will take some time to analyze their transactions whenever another cycle of abandonment, shame, and contempt has been triggered. This, of course, must be done from the objective position offered by the Adult ego-state (also known as *Third Perceptual Position* below).

3.3.2 Perceptual Positions

The Child ego-states will not be able to detach from the emotions and habitual ways of reacting to these cycles. A skill *necessary for growth and change*, then, is the *ability to detach and gain some psychological distance from such emotions*. The **Neuro-Linguistic Programming** (NLP) **Perceptual Positions** offer skills extremely useful in the development of abilities to detach at will.

Perceptual positions have to do with perspectives. The descriptions below outline those perspectives. As you read them, you need to know the terms "association" and "dissociation." In NLP terms, to "associate" means to be in my own body, seeing, hearing and feeling from my own perspective. To "dissociate" means to imagine stepping out of my own body. From there I can do many things: I can imagine stepping into the body (associating) of the person you are interacting with (*second position*), or you can imagine just moving your awareness "over there" somewhere to gain a perspective of an uninvolved observer (*third position*).

In third position you can imagine being an innocent bystander watching what is going on with "those two over there," even speaking in third person. For example, *"She is just trying to get him to see how she feels, and he is too defensive to hear what she is saying. If he would just slow down and listen then she would feel heard, and this would be resolved."* Second position is the position of empathy and third position is the position of objectivity (See descriptions below).

In first and second position you are an actor *"in a movie"* seeing from behind your own eyes (*associated into self*) or the eyes of the other person (*associated into other*). But in third position you are not in the movie at all (*dissociated or detached*). Your awareness is *"out in the auditorium of the theater,"* or floating above the movie like a bird, etc.

Taking time after a conflict to be alone and explore "what just happened" from all three positions can drastically improve our relationships.

Being able to move flexibly in and out of these positions is the ideal. We need first position for self-awareness and boundary setting, we need second position for empathy, and we need third position for objectivity. Notice that we can and do get stuck in one position. Addicts get stuck in first position, codependents get stuck in second position, and people who have totally cut themselves off from their emotions to get stuck in third position.

Perceptual Positions

First position – the *"all about me" position* ,or *position of self-awareness*

- When you associate into your own body, you live in first position.
- You look, feel, and hear the world from your own viewpoint. You are inside your own body, looking out from your own eyes, and hearing from your own ears.
- In first position, you do not take into account anyone else's position. You simply think, "How does this conversation or communication affect me?"
- First Position is the *position of self-awareness* and the Child ego-states which are about *what I want, what I need,* and *what I feel.* Addicts and alcoholics tend to get stuck in

the Child ego-states and become *"like a kid in a candy store without parental supervision."*

Second position – the *"all about others" position,* or *position of empathy*

- This means stepping into the other person's shoes.
- Take into account how the event or communication would look, feel, and sound from another person's point of view.
- Imagine you're entering the other person's body; in this position you imagine looking at yourself through those eyes, hearing yourself from those ears, feeling what it might feel as a result of that.
- What do you look like, sound like, and what feelings do you get from the other person's viewpoint of you?
- This position gives much flexibility when involving conflict with someone.
- Second Position is the *position of empathy* and is extremely valuable for deepening rapport with the other person.
- If we get stuck in the second position, we tend to become totally other-centered and can get stuck in the role of Rescuers and Caretakers to the exclusion of taking care of ourselves (Internalizers/Codependents).

Third position – the *position of "detachment"* or *position of objectivity*

- Dissociate from the entire event or conversation and become an independent observer.
- Third Position allows us to operate from the "position of objectivity," *how would this conversation/event look, sound, and feel to someone totally uninvolved?*
- Imagine yourself being out of your body and off to the side of the conversation between you and the other person; you can see both yourself and the other person "over there."
- Imagine being a bird in a tree above "those two down there," or try the perspective of a "worm's eye view."
- If we get stuck in the third-position, we may take a historical view, cultural view, etc., so that we become so

dissociated from our body and emotions that we seem more like robots than people (*the computer role*).

- Third position is well suited for "detaching" from dysfunctional relationships.

Journal Exercise: Use a separate piece of paper to draw the following diagram and then use it to *analyze two recent conflicts between you and your partner.*

1. Staying in your Adult ego-state (***Third Perceptual Position***), identify the opening comment, the reaction of the other party, and so on.

2. List and number partner A's comments on one side of the diagram, list and number partner B's comments on the other side of the diagram.

3. For each numbered comment draw an arrow diagramming the ego-states involved (sender and receiver). Notice if they remain complementary and what happens if they cross.

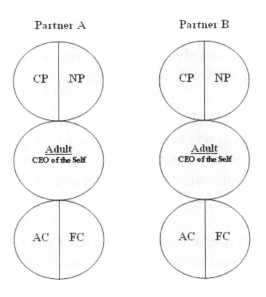

3.3.3 Assertive Communication

Although we all use different communication styles in different situations, we each have a favored style we use the most. Think about you and your partner as you read about the following dysfunctional styles; think about your own habits and those of other people in your life. Keep in mind there are certain contexts when these styles are useful and appropriate (*see examples in parentheses below*).

- **Aggressive Style** Expressing yourself with an attitude of intimidation; little regard for others' rights, thoughts, or feelings; Aggressive communication can be abusive, threatening, and judgmental, and may include name-calling, yelling, interrupting, sarcasm, ridicule, and hostile body language (*appropriate in self-defense situations*)

- **Passive-Aggressive Style** Not expressing yourself openly but, instead, hinting, being indirect, or being silent about what you want, think, or feel; talking behind others' backs; being sarcastic; pouting; whining; constant complaining; expecting others to know what you think, feel, or want without your telling them; refusing to talk even though you're obviously upset (*appropriate when playing Pictionary or other party game*).

- **Passive Style** Not feeling that you have a right to feelings or opinions; don't express yourself in any way that might upset others, or possibly any way at all; giving short, uninformative answers; agreeing with whatever others say (*appropriate if you are in a hostage situation*)

In a healthy relationship, saying what you mean in a way that is respectful both to yourself and to others is a skill that can be learned, and so is hearing what others are trying to share with you. Effective communication requires two basic skills: (1) expressing yourself clearly, and (2) listening actively. *Assertiveness* is the term for this style of communication.

- **Assertive Style** Expressing your thoughts, feelings, and wishes without ignoring those of others; being able to disagree openly and say "no" in a way that respects both others and oneself (*required for authentic Intimacy*)

Journal Exercise: Which of the above communication styles best describes you when having a conflict with your partner? Which style describes your partner? Give an example of how a fight goes between you.

3.4 Feelings & Emotions

Most people use the terms "feelings" and "emotions" interchangeably. However, they are not exactly one-and-the-same. In order to understand the distinction between them it is important to cover a few basics about the "autonomic nervous system" (ANS). The ANS consists of branches of nerves within the "central nervous system" (CNS). Within the ANS are two primary branches of nerve fibers referred to as the "sympathetic nervous system" (SNS), and the para-sympathetic nervous system (PNS). The SNS consists of the "on-switch" and circuitry for the fight-or-flight response. The PNS is the "on-switch" and circuitry for the relaxation response.

The SNS is responsible for preparing the mind-and-body to respond to a threat while the PNS acts to restore homeostasis by returning the body to its accustomed steady-state. Part of the PNS is the vagus nerve, which is the tenth of twelve cranial nerves running from the brain into various parts of the body; in this case, from the mid-brain down the mid-line (thoracic region) of the body; i.e., through the jaw, throat, chest, solar plexus, stomach, into the lower gut right behind the belt buckle, including the genitalia. "Vagus" means "wandering." This wandering nerve branches out through the whole thoracic region, connecting to every vital organ. The primary function of the vagus nerve is to send signals from the vital organs back to the brain so the brain can monitor and regulate them.

Eighty to ninety percent of the fibers in the vagus nerve are *afferent* nerves – meaning they carry information from the organs to the brain. Ten to twenty percent of the fibers are *efferent* nerves – meaning they carry information to the organs from the brain. This suggests that, along with monitoring of the vital organs and homeostatic regulation functions, the vagus nerve is also an important part of an information highway between the mind and body.

A feeling is a physiological sensation that develops somewhere along the mid-line. It may be tightness in the chest, clenching of the teeth, butterflies in the stomach, a lump in the throat, tension in the neck and shoulders, or some other sensation. So a feeling in this sense is a communication coming from the body to the mind. When that physical sensation reaches our awareness (in the mind) it is supposed to trigger a search as if asking the question, "What is that?"

The pre-frontal cortex (the thinking part of brain) does a database search and consults the amygdala, (the feeling part of the brain); it then chooses an answer in the form of an emotional label. When the feeling is assigned a label it becomes an emotion. In the ideal situation, this body-mind communication results in an accurate interpretation of the feeling followed by a suitable response to that communication – either in the form an expression (getting it out, releasing it, sharing it with another person) or in the form of taking some sort of appropriate action (e.g., taking a day off if the emotion, say frustration, is related to working too much).

In a moderate-to-severely dysfunctional family healthy, emotional coping skills were not taught. In fact, the primary rule in a dysfunctional family, even if it is unspoken, is "Don't Feel." When certain needs or feelings began to surface, they had to be ignored, disowned, discounted, repressed or otherwise pushed back out of awareness. Two more general rules we learned to follow are, *"Don't Trust"* and *"Don't Talk"* because the dysfunctional family is not a safe place to do so.

These three rules are important for survival, but they are also powerful contributors to the development of frozen feeling-states. These rules are a direct cause of emotional arrest. One cannot obey these rules and learn to cope with feelings in a healthy way. Emotional coping has to be learned and any learning requires practice. Is it any wonder that we react in child-like ways when triggered into the fight-or-flight mode? Learning to break these rules is a requirement of change.

Developing healthy emotional coping skills to provide an alternative to the skills we learned to survive on the battlefield will be a major focus of healing and recovery. Below is a technique for getting in touch with your feelings and breaking the "no-talk, no-feel" rules. But once you get in touch with those feelings what do you do about it? Steps five through seven are about dealing with the message your feelings have for you.

3.4.1 Seven-Step Feeling Process

1. **Notice the feeling or sensation.** You must first learn to notice the feeling, i.e., the uncomfortable physical sensation.

2. **Identify the location of the feeling or sensation.** Feelings usually reside in one of four major areas of the body: the jaw, neck and shoulders, chest, or stomach. Other parts of the body may also be involved, but the center of it emanates from one of these major areas. Images and sounds may also accompany the signals.

3. **Breathe into that location** focusing all your concentration on it and staying with that feeling or sensation. Experience it, allow it to exist, and ask it to communicate with you.

4. **Ask for and receive the message or positive intention of the feeling or sensation.** Remember that all parts of self and all feelings or sensations in our body have a positive intention for us. These signals or messages are meant to help us remain healthy and protect or preserve our body. Just relax, close your eyes, and ask:

"Would the part of me responsible for this feeling in my (stomach) *please tell me what is your message or positive intention for signaling me this way?"* Then, just wait for an intuitive reply to come to you. Ask more questions if you intuitively feel there is more to discover from this part of you.

5. **Thank that part of you for communicating its needs and feelings.**

6. **Now, make a 24-hour promise to the part.** Tell the part of you that you intend to do something about this message within the next hours. For instance, if the message received is that you're pushing yourself too hard, tell this part that you will take frequent breaks that day and spend time relaxing that evening by taking a bubble bath, watching a movie, or doing something fun.

7. **Notice the feeling fade away.** If your response to the part's message was adequate, the feeling will disappear. This is an indication that your response has been accepted and appreciated.

3.4.2 Ground Rules for Fighting Effectively

Assertive communication can only be conducted with the full power and resources of the logical, objective, *CEO of the Self;* i.e., the *Adult ego-state*. When we get triggered into survival mode the *Angry/Defiant* Child tends to use an *aggressive style (attacking)*, the *Vulnerable/Needy* ego-state tends to use a *passive style (retreating)*, and the *Critical Parent* ego-state tends to use a *passive-aggressive style (defending* and *covert ops)*.

The following are general ground rules for developing an assertive style of communication with your partner. A violation of any of these is a red flag that you have been triggered and are in a Child ego-state ready to play another round of abandonment, shame, and contempt with your partner.

- **No Name-Calling or Put-Downs**
- **Wait Your Turn, Really Listen**
- **Take Your Partner Seriously**
- **Validate Your Partner's Feelings** (even if you don't agree with them)
- **Use Second Perceptual Position to Enhance Empathy** (p.126)
- **Avoid Long Speeches and Take Frequent Turns as Speaker**
- **Be Specific and Stick as Close to the *Here-and-Now* as Possible**
- **One Thing at a Time; Don't Cloud the Issue**
- **Take Ownership of Your Feelings and Actions**
- **Get Feedback; Gather Information**
- **Respond to Both the Verbal and Nonverbal Parts of the Message**
- **Prevent Escalation** (adapted from McKay et al, 1995)

There are three things you can do to prevent escalation; (1) Watch nonverbal behavior, (2) breathe deeply to slow down the pace of the exchange, and (3) declare a "time out."

1. *Stay aware of the nonverbal part of every fight.* Watch for danger signals voices getting louder, threatening gestures, a shift from sitting to standing, pointing fingers, clenching fists, a book slammed down or other objects tossed around or broken, fast pacing, shoving, and so on.

2. *As soon as you notice that you are getting excited, stop talking and take a deep breath.* Just turn away from your partner, inhale deeply into your abdomen, and release the breath slowly and completely in a big sigh. Suggest that your partner do the same to calm down. You are literally

"taking a breather." It calms you down and buys time to think about the rules of fair fighting.

3. *If taking a breather to buy time doesn't work, call a formal "time out."* Time out has very specific rules:

   a. **Agree in advance on a signal**, such as the "T" sign that professional sports referees use to call time out during a game.

   b. **No last words**. As soon as one person calls time out, you both stop talking immediately.

   c. **Leave immediately**. The person who called time out leaves the room or, ideally, the house. If you're in a car or some other place you can't leave, stop talking for a set amount of time. A time out should last about an hour. Stay out of each other's presence the whole time.

   d. **Always return when time's up.**

   e. **Don't use drugs or alcohol during time out.**

   f. **Don't rehearse what you should have said or are going to say**. This will just keep you upset. If possible, get some physical exercise during your time out.

   g. **Check in when you get back**. See if this is a good time to resume. If either of you is still too upset to continue, set a time in the near future to talk again.

- **As the Speaker, Use The Five Elements of a Clear Message:**
  - **I feel/felt** _____ (State your feelings <u>about the topic</u> being discussed at the moment – not about the whole relationship)

o **When I see/heard** _____
(Describe your observations in <u>sensory terms only</u> –
no interpretations, just what you see and hear/heard)

o **Because** _____ (This is
your best guess about what their intention or
communication means, but <u>not a fact until
confirmed by your partner</u>. *You must be able to trust
that your partner is being honest when your
interpretation is confirmed or denied or this is
where the process breaks down. Without trust you
are indeed in trouble and may need outside help.*

o **I want or need** _____ (<u>Your
preferences, desires and needs</u> [boundaries] in this
situation go here)

o **If you do/ don't** _____ (Set your
boundaries about *what you will or won't do* if your
partner agrees and what you will or won't do if your
partner declines to accept your boundary.)

- **As an Active Listener, Confirm the Message You
Received:**

  a. You feel/felt _____ (*Your
  Partner's Feelings*)

  b. When You see/hear _____ (*Your
  Partner's Sensory Data*)

  c. Because _____ (*Your
  Partner's Interpretation*)

d. You want or need _____ (*Your Partner's Requests*)

e. If I do/don't _____ (*Your Partner's Boundaries*)

f. **YOUR RSPONSE**_____ (*Only after your partner confirms* you have received their message correctly)

- **Switch Roles After Completing the Above Two Items.**

- **Beware of Magical Thinking:**
  The Little Professor uses the magical thinking of childhood to get us out of tight spots. The Adult ego-state uses the objective, cause-and-effect thinking.

Magical Thinking Styles of the Little Professor:

1. *Black-and-White Thinking* – Thinking in words like always, never, no one, everyone, every time, everything, etc.

2. *Focusing on the Negative* – Filtering out the good, seeing only the bad in a situation, and magnifying it.

3. *Fortune Telling* – Predicting the worst possible outcome to a situation. *"Doing your pain in advance"* is unnecessary most of the time because it rarely happens.

4. *Mind Reading* – Believing that you know what others are thinking and feeling, even though they haven't told you.

168

5. ***Thinking with Your Feelings*** – Believing negative feelings without ever questioning them: "I feel it, so it must be true." "If I feel stupid, I must be stupid."

6. ***Should/Must Thinking*** – Thinking in words like should, must, ought, or have to. *"Everyone should do things my way." "I ought to be able to control my feelings better."* Don't "should" on yourself!

7. ***Self-Labeling*** – Generalizing one or two qualities into a negative global judgment about you. You don't achieve your goal for two weeks in a row and say to yourself, "I'm a failure."

8. ***Personalizing*** – Investing innocuous events with personal meaning. Thinking that things other people do or say is some kind of a reaction toward you.

9. ***Blaming*** – Blaming someone else for your own pain/problems or go the other way and blame yourself for everyone else's problems.

10. ***Over-Generalizing*** – Coming to a general conclusion based upon a single event or incident. Thinking that when one bad thing happens, it will continue to happen over and over again

11. ***Catastrophizing*** – Expecting disaster, going through the entire list of negative "what ifs" in a situation.

12. ***Control Fallacies*** – If you feel externally controlled, you see yourself as a helpless victim of fate. If you feel internally controlled, you see yourself as responsible for the pain and happiness of everyone around you.

3.5 Moving into Growth-Mode

Moving from Self-Preservation into Self-Actualization means both partners must find a way to set familiar, automatic, survival-oriented coping skills aside (especially any active addictions) to focus on co-creating a new system that leads to growth, both as individuals and as a couple. This means in your search for true intimacy, you must forego the intensity of the games and cycles that produce the Chemistry of Drama. In the long term, this will pay off in a deeply rewarding and satisfying partnership.

As with anything else in the process of change, you will need to adopt the goal of progress, not perfection. Then CELEBRATE the gains you make! starting with the work you have done in this book that brought you up to this point. If you have done the journal exercises in the preceding sections you have accumulated a new level of self-awareness. This is sixty percent of change, so you are already over halfway done!

The following is an outline for healing your relationship and moving from *Survival-Mode* into *Growth-Mode*:

I. Stop the Bleeding! In order to initiate the healing of an injury you must first stop the bleeding. In order to do this you must:

- ASK your partner for a truce or cease fire;

- DECIDE as a couple if you want to turn things around, if yes then

- STOP treating your partner like an enemy (p.146),

- STOP Bradshaw's Four Horseman of the Marital/Relationship Apocalypse (p.141),

- STOP the Chemistry of Drama produced by acting out cycles of abandonment, shame, and contempt (p. 57),

- STOP the endless games of Punishment and Forgiveness (p. 129), Distance & Pursuit (p.117), and the Figure-Eight (p. 86);

- UNDERSTAND this will take commitment and a conscious effort every day to develop a new way of effectively relating to each other, and

- BE WILLING to settle for *"progress – not perfection."*

II. Diagnose Your Condition In order to treat a problem you must first know what the symptoms are and where exactly the damage is. In order to do this you must:

- KNOW YOUR CORE ISSUES (pp. 99-101) and when to get professional help if the wounds are too deep to address on your own – especially if an untreated active addiction, codependency, or other compulsive behaviors are not yet stabilized;

- LEARN about the *Dance of Externalization* also known as The Drama Triangle (p. 117) and the Enabling Trap (p.149),

- LEARN the traits of a healthy relationship (p. 136) so you can identify what areas upon which you need to focus,

- LEARN the normal stages of a healthy relationship (p. 80) so you can identify where you are in the process,

- LEARN the Twenty Signs of Marital and Relationship Problems (p. 141) to identify specific problem areas in your marriage, and

- LEARN the psychological mind games (p.113) you play as a couple and refuse to play along.

II. Apply First Aid Treating your condition also requires learning and using new relationship skills. Remember that the term "relationship" is a nominalization of the action word meaning to "relate." Healthy relating includes:

- **LEARN Healthy Communication Skills**

  o Use the Seven-Step Feelings Process to increase self-awareness and develop healthy emotional skills (p. 172)
  o Use the Functional Ego-State Map for Analyzing Communication (p. 159)
  o Use Assertive Communication (p. 169)
  o Use the Ground Rules for Fighting Assertively (p. 169)
  o Know when to Call Time Out! (p. 175)

- **LEARN The Five Elements of a Clear Message** (p.176):

  o I feel/felt _____ (*Your Feelings*)
  o When I see/hear _____ *(Sensory Data)*
  o Because _____ (*Your Best guess until confirmed*)
  o I want or need _____ (*Your Preferences*)
  o If you do/don't _____ (*Your Boundaries*)

- LEARN how your relationship with yourself affects your relationships with others. Complete *Thawing Adult/Child Syndrome* to develop self-awareness and ***a healthy relationship with yourself first*** so you can have healthy relationships with others.

- LEARN how to set and reinforce Healthy Boundaries (pp.176-177)

- **LEARN how to use the Perceptual *Positions*** (p.165)

  o *First Position* – Identifying and Expressing Your Wants and Needs
  o *Second Position* – Building Rapport and Developing Empathy Skills
  o *Third Position* – Objectivity, detachment and Emotional Regulation Skills

III. Now Actualize Your Relationship!! (Growth Mode)

- **Develop a Long-Term Relationship Plan** (Appendix A)

Appendix A

Actualize Your Relationship!

Develop a Long-Term Plan for Your Future as a Couple: The NLP **Logical Levels of Change** provide a great framework and foundation for building an effective long-term relationship plan. It is recommended that each partner go through the following process **as an individual, then come together** and negotiate using your individual plans to co-create a plan for who you are going to be as a couple!

- *Spirituality* – How do we want to relate to each other spiritually in this relationship?
- *Identity* – What kind of couple do we want to be in this relationship?
- *Values* – What do we deem most important in this relationship?
- *Beliefs* – What do we feel certain about or want to feel certain about in this relationship?
- *Capabilities & Skills* – What are we able to do, or what would we like to be able to do better in this relationship? What skills and resources do we already have that would help us be able do that? What skills and resources do we need to do to acquire or develop? How will we acquire or develop them?
- *Behaviors* – What actions or reactions would we like to keep or change in this relationship?
- *Environment* – What playmates, play places, playthings, and situations do we need to keep/change in this relationship?

Alignment of the NLP Logical Levels of Change

In his book *Changing Belief Systems with NLP*, Robert Dilts (1990) points out that **spirituality** functions to transmit God's will to us, **identity** defines our mission or purpose in life, **values and beliefs** give us the internal permission and motivation to change, our **capabilities and skills** give us directions about how to make the change and what new resources we need to develop in order to do so, our **behaviors** tell us which actions and reactions need to be changed, and in our **environment**, we need to identify the obstacles and barriers which need to be removed in order for us to make the change(see chart below).

Dilts goes on to say that the ideal is to be fully aligned at all levels. He shares a very interesting insight connecting the Logical Levels of Change with the teachings of Jesus Christ. Dilts explains. *When Jesus was challenged to answer what the greatest Commandment was, he jumped to a higher logical level. He didn't say, "Thou shalt not do this or that behavior...He said that the first and most important commandment was "Love your God with your heart, your mind, your soul and your strength...*

When we think of what it means in relationship to the levels we've been exploring, it is saying to organize yourself toward your highest spiritual purpose (God), with your heart (or beliefs and values), your mind (your capabilities), your soul (your identity), your strength (your behavior). Basically there was an alignment of all those levels [italics his]...Jesus also said there was the second Commandment as important as the first, but it came after the first: To love your neighbor as yourself.

Dilts believes that all logical levels need to be fully aligned in order for a person to truly love who they are. How can we love anyone *as we love ourselves* if we don't actually love ourselves? Below is a chart that outlines the alignment of the NLP Logical Levels of Change:

Fully-Aligned Logical Levels of Change

Change?	Level	Function	Area of Focus
(For Whom)	Spirituality	Transmission	*(God)*
(Who)	Identity	Mission/Purpose	*(Soul)*
(Why)	Values & Beliefs	Permission/Motivation	*(Heart)*
(How)	Capabilities & Skills	Directions	*(Mind)*
(What)	Behavior	Actions/Reactions	*(Strength)*
(Where)	Environment	Obstacles & Barriers	*(the world)*

Spirituality: *Whom do I serve and for what purpose?*

The "beyond identity" level connects you with the larger picture when you begin to question your own purpose, ethics, mission, or meaning in life. It brings us to the realms of spirituality and questions of existence. Remember *"whatever's on top runs everything underneath."* This is important because everything we have learned about the Iceberg points to the level of identity as the problem. We have an *invented self, a false self, and the true self* buried underneath all that wounds. This being the case, it's important to go up one level to spirituality in order to change everything underneath. This may be the primary reason why the 12-step programs work so well.

The issues outlined in this book are non-discriminatory. The effects of abandonment, shame and contempt cut across all socio-economic, cultural, racial, political, and other demographic lines – including religious faith. This is because kids are kids no matter where you go; they have the same needs across the globe. How can there be so much sameness in a world with so much diversity?

In many circles, religion and spirituality are not necessarily one-and-the-same. Religion is seen as the practice of a set of beliefs about God and spirituality is simply a daily *personal relationship* with a Higher Power – God as *you* understand God. Prayer and meditation are the skills used to experience that daily personal relationship with one's Higher Power. Remembering that each of us has our own "map of the world," which means there are over seven billion maps of spirituality out there, we can understand why we go out of our way to leave this a personal issue.

Journal Exercise: Explore the following questions as they relate, or don't relate, to you and your relationship:

1. For what reason are you here in the world?
2. What would you like your contribution to be to others?
3. What personal strengths can you add to the bigger world out there?
4. How would you like to be remembered after you die?
5. What greater good do you believe in?
6. How do you wish to express these things in your relationship?
7. How important is God, as you understand God, to your success?

Identity: *Who am I and do I reflect that in the way I live?*

If values can be considered policies for the self, then identity may be considered one's evaluation of one's ability to implement those policies. Based upon the record, we may have either a very positive evaluation of our ability to live up to our own standards, a very negative self-evaluation, or an evaluation somewhere in the middle.

If someone grew up in a highly dysfunctional home he or she may have perceptual or mental filters that suggest he or she will never be good enough. If so, a network of limiting beliefs about one's self programs that person to fail. Addictions are a part of that network, and those beliefs create a self-fulfilling prophecy, proving over and over how *"I will never be good enough"* is "true."

Here are some questions to help you explore your identity. You may not be able to answer some of these questions to your liking yet; most of us have a negatively skewed or biased picture of our identity early in recovery. If you like to be amazed, ask these questions every six months in recovery and record your answers for review each time:

Journal Exercise: Explore the following questions as they relate, or don't relate to you and your relationship:

1. How is what you are experiencing an expression of who you are?
2. What kind of person are you? What are your top eight values?
3. How do you describe yourself? Do you live up to that? How often?
4. What labels do you put on other people?
5. How would others describe you?
6. What is your mission in life? Do you have one?
7. How would you like to see these values expressed in your relationships?

Values & Beliefs: *Why do I make these changes?*

I consider values as fundamental *policies for the self* that define who we are. They direct our lives and yet often we are not even aware of them. What *you* believe to be true is not always what *I* believe to be true. Values are things that are important to us; they are what make us get out of bed in the morning. Things become important to us when we believe they will take us in the direction of that ultimate goal in life – i.e., happiness. It is very difficult to motivate a whole group of people with the same approach. One size does not fit all when it comes to values and beliefs. Values and beliefs drive us and influence the lower levels of capability, behavior, and environment. These are what give us internal *permission* to change.

As already mentioned, the number one value in the lives of addicts is their unhealthy relationship with their object or activity of choice – whatever they trusted to distract them from their inner pain. This is most evident when these people make a list of their values then asks themselves if they have ever done anything to violate any of those values as a result of engaging with that object or activity. For example, a work-addicted, drug-addicted, or shopping-addicted person might say the most important thing is their spouse. However, upon closer examination, they invariably find that they have broken many promises to change to that most important person.

Serious problems arise when our values are in conflict with each other. When addiction becomes the number one value in our life for instance, every other thing that's important to us can be negatively affected. It is very often the case that many people actually lose things that are important to them as a consequence of their addiction. Some have lost everything, including their lives.

I have met many people in my work as a counselor who have lost total faith in themselves as a result of these losses. However, they continue to use that object or engage in that activity to medicate their pain. Many people have said to me, *"I don't think I have any values anymore."* This is an easy thing to challenge in the newly recovering person.

Most people believe that guilt is an indictment against their character. I believe an addict's guilt is actually a testimony to his character. I usually ask him to tell me five things he feels guilty about so I can tell him five good things about himself. For example, when someone tells me she feels guilty about disappointing her parents I tell her that she values being a good daughter. When someone tells me he's feel guilty about hurting his wife or children I tell him he values being a good husband and father.

When people feels guilty, it's an indication that they are breaking *their own* rules, they are not living up *their own* standards of conduct. Like pain, guilt tells us when we are headed in the wrong direction. Guilt is a specific form of pain that tells us when our behavior is out of sync with our values. Behavior describes what one does; values describe who one is as a person. When values and behaviors are out of sync, as they frequently and increasing are in addiction, it means something is very wrong. As an addiction progresses, values and behavior to get further and further out of sync with each other. In recovery, we must work to identify and live up to our values.

Journal Exercise: Explore the following questions as they relate, or don't relate to you and your relationship:

1. Why did I do that? Why did they do that?
2. What factors are important to me in this situation?
3. What is important to the other people in my life?
4. What do I believe to be right and wrong?
5. What has to be true for me to get what I want?
6. When do I say "must" or "should" and "must not" or "should not?"
7. What are my beliefs about this person or situation? Are these beliefs helpful? What beliefs might help me get better results?
8. What would someone I admire believe if they were in my shoes?

Capabilities & Skills: *How do I make these changes?*

These include the skills and abilities that we currently possess and those that we need but have not yet acquired that will help us get the changes we want. Once we have identified and learned the new skills, we must repetitively practice them to gain competence and mastery. These new skills are the building blocks for our new neural network of recovery.

Some examples of skills we already possess may be stubbornness and creativity. Our worst liability can be our best asset. For example, the stubbornness employed in the fight against giving up an addiction can be turned around and used for persistence in recovery. Likewise, the creativity it required to hold things together in the midst of an addiction can be turned around to find ways to support our recovery and even make it fun.

A good example of a crucial new skill is developing the ability to cope with feelings in a healthy way. Addiction has often been referred to as a *feelings disease* because most people who have an addiction become emotionally arrested when they begin to rely on their object or activity of choice to make them feel better; usually somewhere in our teen years. As mentioned earlier, those of us who grew up in a dysfunctional family system were not taught healthy emotional coping skills. They were subject to certain unspoken family rules, such as *"Don't Trust,"" "Don't Talk,"* and *"Don't Feel."* All three of these rules must be broken and replaced with new skills such as the **ability** to trust, talk, and process feelings.

In order to learn the new skills we need, we must first know what they are and where to find them. This helps us understand why going to meetings and being around other people in recovery is one of the most important new habits we must develop. At these recovery meetings, we listen to the *experience, strength,* and *hope* of others who have been where we are. Since we all have our own map of the world, there is a lot of diversity in the perspectives being shared at recovery meetings – we simply take what we need and leave the rest.

The ideas, values, experiences, and beliefs of those who have "been there and done that" provide us with much needed "how-to" information that did not get installed in our family-of-origin. We learn such things as trusting, reaching out to others, what it's like to feel safe in a group, self-disclosure, being accepted for who we are, being loved even before we can love ourselves – the experience of healthy intimacy. These people become our *new pseudo-family* where "everybody knows our name." In a relatively short period of time, the meetings begin to feel like home. They teach us a multitude of recovery-oriented coping skills that are essential to giving ourselves a chance at a better life. We will discuss some of these skills in depth throughout the remainder of this book.

We must also read recovery literature specific our issue in order to gain the knowledge necessary to achieve and maintain recovery. How many books and pamphlets do we digest when we discover we have a serious illness such as heart disease? It is no different here. We need to learn everything possible about healing abandonment, shame and contempt. Anything we take in repeatedly becomes part of us no matter how many ways we hear it or read it – in fact, the more the better!

Prayer and/or meditation are also some of the most important recovery skills we need to develop. We have learned to rely on something outside ourselves for comfort and relief; we may have lost touch with our Higher Power, which is the main source of our ability to generate comfort from within. Internal comfort is also known as serenity; just the opposite of chronic stress.

Studies have indicated that people who are addicted to alcohol and other drugs and those who grew up in moderate-to-severely dysfunctional families have trouble creating alpha waves in their brain (relaxation response). There are many ways to teach your brain to create these important brainwaves such as guided imagery, hypnosis, relaxation training, soothing background sounds, and aroma therapy, to name a few. Notice that all of these methods involve the use of our sensory input channels (*seeing, hearing, touching, smelling, and tasting*). It is important to include them in your daily routine as much as possible.

Journal Exercise:

1. What capabilities and skills do I already possess that will help me in healing my relationships?
2. Which of the capabilities and skills outlined in this book do I/we need to learn and practice in my/our life and relationship?
3. What other capabilities and skills do I need to acquire in order to be happy and successful in this relationship?

Behavior: *What do I need to change?*

In NLP terms, "behavior" refers to what we think about as well as our actions. When one is addicted to an object or activity, thoughts frequently evolve into actions. When one has a well-established addiction network what do you suppose the addict spends the majority of time thinking about? Each time the addiction network is activated, they begin thinking about their object or activity of choice; those thoughts progress to fantasy, fantasy to obsession, obsession to compulsion, and compulsion to *acting-out*.

Upon a review of the *Punishment/Forgiveness Cycle* (p. 98), the compatibility of a Codependent and an Addicted becomes clear; the Codependent is the *punisher* and the (drug, sex, spending, eating, working) Addicted person is the *punishee*.

Codependency is often referred to as an "addiction to the outside" such as having an obsession with a "problem-other."

This description exposes a need to avoid the experience of emotional pain by maintaining an external focus through a set of behaviors such as those outlined in the *Drama Triangle* (p. 89). These are just some of the actions that maintain and support the addictive lifestyle where both people have become dependent. The *Figure 8* (p. 86), *the Enabling Trap* (p. 149), and *Distance & Pursuit* (p. 46) should also be on this list of descriptions.

Another problem is not in the behaviors we choose, but in the behaviors that seem to choose us. How many of us have experienced feeling mad at ourselves while saying *"Why do I always do that!"* or *"Man, I hate it when I do that!"*? It seems like someone or something pushes just the right button, and I do something that I did not consciously decide to do. If I find myself in this situation, then I can know I have just identified an unconscious neural network containing a habitual response to a certain cue or trigger.

Finally, on the topic of behaviors, our neural networks are laden with a multitude of attitudes, beliefs, and behaviors that have been designed to support our addiction. We have NOT had recovery-oriented behaviors and attitudes installed. These will have to be learned, practiced, and then practiced again so we can establish, grow, and maintain a neural net for recovery.

Journal Exercise:

1. What actions and reactions do I already possess that will help me in healing my relationships?
2. Which of the actions and reactions outlined in this book do I/we need to replace in my/our life and relationship?
3. What other behaviors do I need to acquire in order to be happy and successful in this relationship?

Environment: *Where do I need to change?*

When we are experiencing pain in our lives we often have an instinct to blame someone or something "out there" in our environment for the problem. For example, have you ever heard this statement, *"If you would quit doing that, I wouldn't have to feel this way."* Or this one: *"If my boss would get off my back, I could do much better at work."* Or these: *"If I had more money, I could go to college. Then I wouldn't be trapped in this crummy job,"* and *"If we didn't live in this boring town, I wouldn't have to drink."*

Our "environment" is anything outside of our own skin, including other people, activities, obligations, children, etc. Even though our environment may be the *easiest* level to make a change that does not mean it is easy to change it – change may come hard at any level. In the case of addiction the environment is where we have built the *external* networks over the years that have supported our unhealthy relationships with our objects and activities of choice. These external networks of people, places, and things have become our pseudo-family and familiar, home-like environment. Many times we are as addicted to the lifestyle that supports our addictions as we are the objects and activities of our choice. What dreams do you share about house and home?

In the case of the workaholic, his home environment includes a special workstation in the house and/or a list of "must get to" projects outside the house for the times when he does come home from work. Email, cell phones, and text messaging make it easier to stay in touch with his pseudo-family or network of enablers that help him act-out his addiction.

Journal Exercise:

1. What resources in my environment do I already possess that will help me in healing my relationships?
2. Which of the environmental obstacles outlined in this book do I/me need to replace in my/our life and relationship?
3. What other environmental resources do I need to acquire in order to be happy and successful in this relationship?

Congratulations!

You have completed *Thawing Toxic Relationships* and now have a blueprint for co-creation of a healthy relationship. Don't be afraid to ask for help in making these changes. Sometimes our mental programming can be stubborn and further help is needed. Be sure to check out my website at www.internet-of-the-mind.com for further resources – Including personal coaching services when needed.

Appendix B
Suggested Readings and References

Don Carter (2010) THAW – *Freedom from Frozen Feelings*

Don Carter (2010) *Thawing Childhood Abandonment*

Don Carter (2011) *Thawing Adult/Child Syndrome*

Don Carter (2008) www.Internet-of-the-Mind.com

Don Carter (2008) Thawing the Iceberg Online Memberships at memberships.Internet-of-the-Mind.com

Ian Stewart & Vann Joines (1996) TA Today; *A New Introduction to Transactional Analysis*

John Bradshaw (2005) *Healing the Shame that Binds You*

Charles L. Whitfield (1987) *Healing the Child Within: Discovery and Recovery for Adult Children of Dysfunctional Families*

Charles L. Whitfield (1990) *A Gift to Myself: A Personal Workbook and Guide to "Healing the Child Within"*

Charles L. Whitfield (1991) *Co-Dependence – Healing the Human Condition*

Pia Mellody, Andrea Wells Miller, and J. Keith Miller (1992) *Facing Love Addiction: Giving Yourself the Power to Change the Way You Love*

Pia Mellody, Andrea Wells Miller, and J. Keith Miller (1989) *Facing Codependence: What It Is, Where It Comes from, How It Sabotages Our Lives*

Pia Mellody and Lawrence S. Freundlich (2004) *The Intimacy Factor: The Ground Rules for Overcoming the Obstacles to Truth, Respect, and Lasting Love*

Abraham Maslow (1968) *Toward a Psychology of Being*

Matthew Linn, Sheila Fabricant, and Dennis Linn (1988) *Healing the Eight Stages of Life*

Sharon Wegscheider-Cruse (1991) *The Family Trap: No one escapes from a chemically dependent family*

John Joseph Powell (1995) *Why Am I Afraid to Tell You Who I Am? Insights into Personal Growth*

Rick Warren (2002, 2007) *The Purpose Driven Life*

Craig Nakken (1996) *The Addictive Personality: Understanding the Addictive Process and Compulsive Behavior*

Melody Beattie (1992) *Codependent No More: How to Stop Controlling Others and Start Caring for Yourself*

Claude Steiner (1994) *Scripts People Live: Transactional Analysis of Life Scripts*

Eric Berne (1996) *Games People Play: The Basic Handbook of Transactional Analysis*

AAWS (2002) Alcoholics Anonymous: *The Story of How Many Thousands of Men and Women Have Recovered from Alcoholism*

Terence T. Gorski and Merlene Miller (1986) *Staying Sober: A Guide for Relapse* Terence T. Gorski (1997) *Prevention by Passages through Recovery: An Action Plan for Preventing Relapse*

Robert Dilts (1990) *Changing Belief Systems with NLP*

Daniel G. Amen (2002) *Healing ADD: The Breakthrough Program That Allows You to See and Heal the 6 Types of ADD*

Helen H. Watkins and John G. Watkins (1997) *Ego States: Theory and Therapy*

L. Michael Hall and Barbara P. Belnap (2004) *Sourcebook of Magic: A Comprehensive Guide to NLP Change Patterns*

Made in United States
Troutdale, OR
11/09/2023

14429691R00110